BESTSELLING
BOOK SERIES

Feng Shui Your Workspace For Dummies®

Cheat Sheet

Ten Chi Enhancers

Enhancer	What it does
Color	Colors represent the Five Elements and the Nine Life Sectors on the Bagua. Choose the colors you love best to enhance chi.
Mirrors	Mirrors enhance and reflect chi, energizing areas where they're located. The bigger the better!
Lighting	Candles, natural sunlight, and lamps all bring more chi into an environment and brighten up your surroundings.
Crystals	Crystals can slow chi down and speed it up, depending on what's needed. Hang them in windows, above doors, and in dark corners. Choose round, multifaceted leaded crystals.
Sound	Use wind chimes and bells near entrances to alert you to visitors and to encourage good chi to enter.
Plants	Plants and flowers enhance the chi in an environment. Choose plants that are inviting, without thorns or spiky leaves.
Water features	Feng Shui fountains and aquariums can attract chi. Choose flowing water if you want to encourage abundance!
Natural objects	Objects that you find in nature, like rocks and seashells, often have personal meaning, and raise the positive chi in your environment.
Moving objects	Mobiles, banners, flags, and other objects that move in the wind attract chi and can be used inside or outside your workspace.
Artwork	Even the picture your kid drew in preschool qualifies as artwork. Any type of art that speaks to your heart makes for powerful chi!

Feng Shui Your Workspace For Dummies®

Cheat Sheet

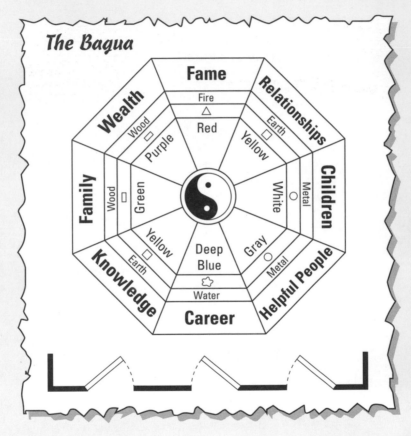

The Bagua

Copyright © 2003 Wiley Publishing, Inc.
All rights reserved.

Item 1987-5.

For more information about Wiley Publishing, call 1-800-762-2974.

For Dummies: Bestselling Book Series for Beginners

Feng Shui Your Workspace

FOR DUMMIES®

Feng Shui Your Workspace

FOR DUMMIES®

by Holly Ziegler
and Jennifer Lawler

WILEY

Wiley Publishing, Inc.

Feng Shui Your Workspace For Dummies®

Published by
Wiley Publishing, Inc.
909 Third Avenue
New York, NY 10022
www.wiley.com

For general information on our other products and services or to obtain technical support, please contact our Customer Care Department within the U.S. at 800-762-2974, outside the U.S. at 317-572-3993, or fax 317-572-4002.

Wiley also publishes its books in a variety of electronic formats. Some content that appears in print may not be available in electronic books.

Library of Congress Cataloging-in-Publication Data:

Library of Congress Control Number: 2003101891

ISBN: 0-7645-1987-5

1B/RR/QW/QT/IN

Manufactured in the United States of America

10 9 8 7 6 5 4 3 2 1

About the Authors

Holly Ziegler is passionate about Feng Shui and is a writer, consultant, and instructor on the subject. Since 1976, she is also a multi-million-dollar real estate broker on California's Central Coast and recently authored *Sell Your Home FASTER with Feng Shui* (Dragon Chi Pub). Somewhere in the midst of this she finds time to fulfill numerous public speaking requests and teach Feng Shui at the college level. Holly lives in the delightful town of Arroyo Grande, California, and is the proud mother of two great kids.

Jennifer Lawler is a freelance writer and martial artist. Holly, using the principles of Feng Shui, has taught her that she would enjoy work more if her desk didn't face the toilet. (And you thought Feng Shui was complicated!) Jennifer writes extensively about martial arts and personal empowerment and is the author of twenty published books, including *Martial Arts For Dummies* (Wiley Publishing, Inc.) and *Dojo Wisdom* (Penguin). She lives in Lawrence, Kansas with her adorable daughter and two rambunctious dogs.

Dedication

Holly dedicates this book to her mentor Denise Linn, who inspires and encourages her at every opportunity.

Jennifer dedicates this book to Vickie Anderson, who got her interested in Feng Shui in the first place.

Acknowledgments

The authors would like to thank Tracy Boggier, acquisitions editor extraordinaire, who has helped and supported them on this project from the very beginning. Tonya Cupp, our project editor, also deserves our thanks for never ever losing patience with us even when we deserved it. Our agent, Carol Susan Roth, has always been a treasure and a dream to work with, and we could not have put this book together without her help. We would also like to thank the technical editor Mark Skinner.

Holly gives a special thank you to Kerry Randall for his on-call continuing guidance and perception; Terry Berryhill and Jack Mallory, her two awesome real estate brokers for the laughter and support through the trying times; Jan Hayes, who makes her way smooth at every opportunity; and Arlene Winn who still keeps her silly and sane.

And, as usual, Jennifer extends her appreciation to her instructors at New Horizons Black Belt Academy of Tae Kwon Do, Mr. Donald Booth and Mrs. Susan Booth, without whom she would still be teaching English for a living.

Namaste,

Holly Ziegler and Jennifer Lawler

Publisher's Acknowledgments

We're proud of this book; please send us your comments through our Dummies online registration form located at www.dummies.com/register/.

Some of the people who helped bring this book to market include the following:

Acquisitions, Editorial, and Media Development

Project Editor: Tonya Maddox Cupp

Acquisitions Editor: Tracy Boggier

Copy Editors: Jennifer Bingham, Chad Sievers

Acquisitions Coordinator: Holly Gastineau Grimes

Technical Editor: Mark Skinner

Senior Permissions Editor: Carmen Krikorian

Editorial Manager: Christine Meloy Beck

Editorial Assistant: Melissa Bennett

Cover Photo: Getty Image

Cartoons: Rich Tennant, www.the5thwave.com

Production

Project Coordinator: Maridee Ennis

Layout and Graphics: Carrie Foster, Joyce Haughey, LeAndra Johnson, Michael Kruzil, Kristin McMullan, Tiffany Muth, Julie Trippetti

Special Art: Illustrations by Kelly Pulley, Photographs by Dena Friesen, Jennifer Lawler, and Holly Ziegler

Proofreaders: John Tyler Connoley, Brian Walls, TECHBOOKS Production Services

Indexer: TECHBOOKS Production Services

Publishing and Editorial for Consumer Dummies

> **Diane Graves Steele,** Vice President and Publisher, Consumer Dummies
>
> **Joyce Pepple,** Acquisitions Director, Consumer Dummies
>
> **Kristin A. Cocks,** Product Development Director, Consumer Dummies
>
> **Michael Spring,** Vice President and Publisher, Travel
>
> **Brice Gosnell,** Publishing Director, Travel
>
> **Suzanne Jannetta,** Editorial Director, Travel

Publishing for Technology Dummies

> **Andy Cummings,** Vice President and Publisher, Dummies Technology/General User

Composition Services

> **Gerry Fahey,** Vice President of Production Services
>
> **Debbie Stailey,** Director of Composition Services

Contents at a Glance

Table of Contents

Introduction

● ●

Say you're at your desk at work. Take a look around. What do you see? If what you see makes you shudder, then this book is for you. Even if it doesn't make you shudder, this book is for you. (We've covered all the angles.)

You've maybe heard something about Feng Shui making an environment more comfortable, but have no idea how it might help you with the plain, drab, utilitarian office you inhabit for so many of your waking hours. *Feng Shui* (pronounced *fung-schway*) is an ancient Chinese philosophy of design that can be applied to any room, building, or desktop. It's mainly about how your space makes you *feel* — often on a subtle, energetic level.

It's not magical except in the way it changes your relationship to your environment. It doesn't require esoteric beliefs. (You don't even have to believe in it for it to work.) Feng Shui is simply a way of looking at the world around you, and rearranging it in a more pleasing pattern . . . one that makes you feel good.

About This Book

You've got a workspace (or you wouldn't have picked this book up in the first place) and it needs some help (or you wouldn't have picked this book up in the first place). Fortunately, you've come to the right place.

This book gives you tried-and-true methods for fixing the challenges in your workspace (including difficult co-workers!). We cover the basic principles of Feng Shui and show you how to use those principles in a variety of environments. We give you tips on curing imbalances, blocked energy, and other problems (like difficult co-workers). You can discover how to spot problems that contribute to workplace tensions and find out how to solve them.

Conventions Used in This Book

We sometimes use foreign words and terms you may not have encountered before. When this happens, we *italicize* the term the first time we use it, and then give you a definition.

Whenever we talk about a subject we've covered more thoroughly elsewhere, we tell you where by naming the chapter ("See Chapter 9 for more information"). This helps keep us from repeating ourselves over and over again. Trust us, you'll be glad we did it this way. We direct you to photographs and drawings in a similar way. *See Figure 1-2* means to look at the second illustration in Chapter 1 for an example of what we're talking about. The illustration mentioned is labeled Figure 1-2.

Foolish Assumptions

We assumed some things about you as we wrote this book:

- ✔ You have a job.
- ✔ You want to do well in your career.
- ✔ You think your surroundings could be more attractive.

How This Book Is Organized

Yes, there is a method to our madness. We've organized this book in such a way as to make the information easy to find and easy to use (at least we think it's easy to find and easy to use and we hope you agree).

Part 1: Reading Feng Shui's Resume

In Part I we discuss the basic principles of Feng Shui. We define key terms such as *chi, Bagua, yin-yang* and *the Five Elements*. We also give background information on the various schools of Feng Shui, including Tibetan Black Sect, which is the school of thought this book follows (as does its companion text, *Feng Shui For Dummies* [Wiley Publishing, Inc.]).

We show you how to develop Feng Shui eyes (and we explain why you should). We show you how to understand the movement of chi, and how to keep from blocking it, and we give you a basic strategy for dealing with design challenges, starting with busting clutter and rearranging the furniture.

We also show how all of the principles of Feng Shui work together and how you can apply them to your specific workspace. We solve some of your design problems by explaining how to cure common Feng Shui challenges. And we finish up by revealing the power of intention.

Part II: Conceptualizing and Strategizing: Oddly at Peace with Peace

We show how to apply the principles of Feng Shui to any workspace — in other words, this could be called "Feng Shui in Action." We include basic techniques and give information on lighting, plants, and flowers. We also give you tools to counteract oppressive elements like overhead beams and too much metal. We explain the importance of color and texture in Feng Shui. We also cover the challenges of electronic equipment in designing a comfortable, welcoming workspace.

Part III: Energizing and Feng Shui-ing Your Work Area

We get down to brass tacks here, giving you the low-down on handling specific workspaces, whether you work out of a traditional office or the floor of a machine shop. Here, you'll find the information you need to know to

- Build a Feng Shui-friendly building from the get-go
- Make your cubicle/open concept office/home office/car/ countertop comfortable
- Bring Feng Shui with you when you're on the go
- Spruce up those rooms that get ignored in every office building

Part IV: Interacting with Others: Implementing for Success

Feng Shui can enhance your career success. In this part we show you how to do so and show the connection between Helpful People and Wealth. Feng Shui can help you take control in your work and meet your goals, no matter what they are; we help you do that, too.

Part V: The Part of Tens

In this part, we give you four top-ten lists for quick reference. We show you how to fix common workplace problems the Feng Shui way, we give you the low-down on increasing your wealth using

Feng Shui tactics, and we give you pointers on improving your relationships with your co-workers (techniques you can also use with your boss and clients). And take a look at the Appendix, because we've created some blank workspace forms, so that you can sketch your workspace with ease.

Icons Used in This Book

In the margins of the book, we use several different icons to identify material that you can use to better understand and apply the principles of Feng Shui:

This icon warns you that a certain strategy, placement or approach is *not* good Feng Shui and should be avoided as unfavorable. This icon also alerts you to potential health or safety troubles. Pay attention.

This icon is used to indicate important Feng Shui principles, especially how to apply them to your particular situation. If you know nothing else, try to recall this stuff.

This icon highlights suggestions that make your workspace the best, most comfortable it can be.

This icon points out stuff that's interesting, but definitely not crucial to using Feng Shui. Skip it if you want, dive right in if you prefer.

Where to Go from Here

You don't have to read front to back in this book. So where to go?

- ✔ If you're a Feng Shui novice, turn to Chapter 1, "Figuring Out Feng Shui" for information on the basics.

- ✔ If you want to brush up on the basics but aren't a beginner, turn to Chapter 2, "Moving and Grooving with Chi."

- ✔ If you're trying to find a solution to your electronic equipment troubles, find Chapter 6, "Zoning In on Electronic Equipment."

- ✔ If you have a Feng Shui background and want to get right to solving the design challenges, turn to Part 3 and choose the chapter that applies to your workspace. For example, Chapter 10 is for corner-office-dwellers, whereas Chapter 11 is for home office workers.

Part I
Reading Feng Shui's Resume

The 5th Wave   By Rich Tennant

"It was Jack's idea to have a home office, but I picked out the artwork to relax him while he's working."

In this part . . .

Feng Shui teaches you to see your environment in a new light and clear your mind — along with all that clutter!

In this part, we introduce you to some basic concepts of Feng Shui that we use throughout the book. We also give you some background on where Feng Shui came from and how it developed.

We overview the basic principles behind Feng Shui, help you apply those principles to your workspace, and take a look at how the different principles interact with and support each other. You can also find out about the power of intention.

Chapter 1

Figuring Out Feng Shui

● ●

In This Chapter

▶ Walking the balance beam with Feng Shui

▶ Going over a few good schools of Feng Shui

▶ Figuring out the basics

▶ Putting it all together

▶ Using your intentions positively

● ●

The ancient wisdom of Feng Shui applied to your workspace can make you feel more comfortable during working hours. It can help you get along with that difficult and challenging co-worker, make you more productive and efficient at your work-related tasks, and can even help you play well with others. Not a bad day's work for what's basically a design philosophy!

Getting along Famously: Balance and Harmony

Feng Shui literally means *wind and water,* referring to the two universal forces necessary for life. These universal elements are connected to *chi,* which is life energy or life force. Wind and water carry this life energy throughout the world. Feng Shui shows you how to harness this life energy to enrich your environment and create balance in your life. See the section, "Flowing Like Chi" later in the chapter for more information on chi. Chapter 2 talks about chi at length.

Feng Shui, a classic Chinese philosophy of design, is something between an art and a science. It brings balance, blessings, and abundance to a space through harmonious placement and use of appropriate design elements.

Creating balance and harmony is the essential purpose of Feng Shui. If your environment is in balance, you will feel comfortable and welcome there. That's the important thing — how your environment makes you feel. Feng Shui principles show that when any element in a design is out of balance — too much of one element and not enough of another (see Figure 1-1), or the elements are in conflict with each other — then *you* feel out of balance. Without balance you don't have harmony. In other words, you've got the Feng Shui blues. But don't worry. We have the cure for you.

Feng Shui emphasizes our basic interconnection with nature. At its core, it's about living in harmony with our environment. When we are in harmony with our environment we are happier and more productive! That's why you should Feng Shui your workspace.

Feng Shui affects your material success, your health (physical, mental and emotional), and your relationships with others. It does all this even if you pay no attention to where your desk is positioned. If your desk is in the right spot, more power (literally) to you. If it's in the wrong spot, look out: Even if you don't pay attention negative energy can leave you feeling ungrounded and less than powerful. Of course this affects your productivity and wealth!

The staircase dominates the room.

The plants are a good attempt at balance but insufficient.

Figure 1-1: This entryway is dominated by one element — Wood.

Applying Feng Shui's principles to your workspace doesn't have to be complicated, time-consuming, or expensive. And the rewards are well worth any time and energy you spend.

Showing What Feng Shui Can Do for You

All that talk about balance and harmony is fine, but bottom line: What does Feng Shui do for you? It can make you more productive, which is good for your career. Case in point: in Feng Shui, order is a prime principle and clutter is banished. You can easily imagine that being more organized will make it easier to do your work. Or how about this: Facing the entrance to your workspace (a Feng Shui golden rule) allows you to anticipate what's going to happen next. You'll actually be able to see what's coming instead of being surprised when the boss taps you on the shoulder. Being prepared can't hurt your career.

But that's not all. Feng Shui also helps you accomplish your career goals in another way. As you design your space according to the principles of Feng Shui, you create and use *intentions* — stating what you want to accomplish by making these changes. You use Feng Shui principles with awareness and thought. If you decide to place your desk in a more favorable position, it's because you intend to be more successful in your career. That intention is extremely powerful.

Making efficiency with an ounce of prevention

We know, we know, it seems like it might take some energy and time to transform your workspace into Feng Shui central. And it might get a little complicated, especially when you can't figure out which way to turn the Bagua, or when you find out that what you thought was the Wealth sector was actually the Children sector all along, which explains why your son won the Lotto and why you didn't get the raise you were looking for. Chapter 3 can help you get that stuff straight.

Relax. Take a deep breath. Feng Shui takes exactly as much time and energy as you want to give it. And spending some time upfront will save you time (and energy and frustration) in the long run. If you don't have a lot of time right now, just start with a small, fundamental change, like clearing the clutter out of your office. This alone helps you feel better and energetically lighter. See Chapter 2 for more information on clutter busting.

And even if you do make a mistake, you can easily correct it. You're making positive changes and are on the right track!

Getting what you want

The beauty of Feng Shui is that it can help you achieve your goals (in addition to perking up your workspace). Every time you place an object so that it enhances a Life Sector, you're creating and maintaining an intention — you're trying to get closer to your goals. Chapter 3 talks more about these things: so crucial to Feng Shui's success!

Intentions help you

- ✔ **Set goals:** Goals that are important to you, not to anyone else.

- ✔ **Focus:** When you decide to do some work in your Career sector for example, you can take the steps you need toward success.

- ✔ **Clear clutter:** Not only do you clear the clutter out of your workspace, but in doing so it helps you clear the clutter out of your mind.

Allow myself to introduce myself . . .

Feng Shui helps you discover yourself and what is important to you. Contemplating the Nine Life Sectors and considering which ones are most important to you right now gives you insight, as does thinking about your intentions. In addition, seeing the world with *Feng Shui eyes* — with a perception attuned to the principles of Feng Shui — requires you to reflect on what you think and feel.

As you settle into Feng Shui, don't dismiss the sensation when a room makes you feel uncomfortable. Analyze it, discovering what in your environment causes the sensation. You get more in tune with your feelings and your intuition. (For help on that flip to Chapter 3.) You become more connected with your environment. Feng Shui doesn't just help you decide where to put your credenza. It helps you grow as a person.

Going to Design School

According to legend, Feng Shui originated in approximately 2900 BC, during the reign of Emperor Fu Hsi, who is said to have created the pattern of line symbols that make up the trigrams of the *I Ching*, or *Book of Changes*, the oldest book in China. The distinct pattern of the numbers that emerged is called the lo-shu, or Magic Square (see Figure 1-2), and provides the foundation for Chinese numerology, astrology, and Feng Shui.

4	9	2
3	5	7
8	1	6

Figure 1-2: First the magic bean, then the Magical Mystery Tour, and now: The Magic Square.

The earliest forms of Feng Shui combined figuring out auspicious placement for graves of revered ancestors and for temples, palaces, and imperial buildings. Over time, Feng Shui developed into several specific styles called *schools*.

Kan Yu: The early Feng Shui masters

Kan Yu was the term used for the Feng Shui masters of old who were called upon to determine the most auspicious placement for a grave. The ancient Chinese believed they had a direct connection with their ancestors, so if parents and grandparents were resting comfortably and happily, they bestowed blessings and good fortune on their children and grandchildren. The ideal burial site had mild breezes and rich land; the preferred entrance to a burial site faced south (into the sun) so that the strong winds and nasty weather coming from the north were avoided. These principles became the early foundation of the Feng Shui we practice today.

Gee, Nancy! Tell me about geomancy

Early Feng Shui masters advised people on the best places to build homes and other structures. These experts assessed the energy or *chi* they felt in the land. They considered how harsh the forces of nature were in a given location, how the area might be subject to strong winds or erosion, and took note of the symbolic shape of the land. They observed the land for signs of healthy plants and animals, good, free-flowing water, and rich soil. Rocky outcroppings, dry waterways, and little plant life were all signs of areas to be avoided. This early science of studying the earth was called *geomancy,* and it eventually developed into the environmental design science we understand today as Feng Shui.

Form school

The *Form school,* sometimes called the *Landform school,* is one of the oldest approaches to Feng Shui. In this school the best locations for living and working are determined by looking at the land itself and recognizing its shapes, climate, and other related natural conditions. If you lived in a mountainous area, for example, it's most favorable to have the back of your house to the mountain. In the background, the mountain gives your home a feeling of stability, but if you have to look at it very up close and personal from your front door every day, you may start feeling a little hemmed in.

Compass school

The *Compass school* relies on an understanding of Chinese astrology (based on the *I Ching* described earlier in this section). Particularly important are the directions — or more precisely, the *energies* of the eight directions. Yes, we said eight directions. And you thought four was enough. The Compass school adds northeast, northwest, southeast, and southwest.

Your *personal life directions* (otherwise known as your most favorable directions) are determined using a specific formula, and ideally your space is designed so that it aligns with your most auspicious personal direction. If your best direction is north, then sleeping with your head facing north is considered auspicious. The timing of your birthday is also crucial in this approach to Feng Shui.

Identifying your Celestial Animals

Chinese astrology is similar to Western astrology in that it is believed that people born at certain times share certain personal characteristics and traits. However, a cycle of 12 animals is used and one animal rules each year. See Table 1-1 to figure out what kind of animal you are.

Your Celestial Animal and directions predict your personality type and give clues about how you will behave under various conditions. The best directions would guide you how to sit or face when making important decisions, negotiating contracts, and the like. These are directions of empowerment. Conversely, your worst directions would be where you do not want to face in important situations.

Table 1-1 **A Horse Is a Horse, of Course:
The Celestial Animals Chart**

You're such a	When were you born?	Tell me a little about yourself	Can you send a picture?
Rat	1936, 1948, 1960, 1972, 1984, 1996	The Rat is associated with the element of Water and is most compatible with the Dragon and the Monkey. The Rat is an opportunist devoted to family, sociable but sometimes petty.	
Ox	1937, 1949, 1961, 1973, 1985, 1997	The Ox is associated with the element of Earth and is most compatible with the Snake and the Rooster. The Ox is reliable, sturdy, organized, methodical, and slow to forgive.	
Tiger	1938, 1950, 1962, 1974, 1986, 1998	The Tiger is associated with the element of Wood and is most compatible with the Horse and the Dog. The Tiger is impulsive and easily distracted; naturally enthusiastic; Tigers take failure hard.	

(continued)

Table 1-1 *(continued)*

You're such a	When were you born?	Tell me a little about yourself	Can you send a picture?
Rabbit	1939, 1951, 1963, 1975, 1987, 1999	The Rabbit is associated with the element of Wood and is most compatible with the Goat and the Pig. The Rabbit avoids conflict and is diplomatic. Rabbits may seem docile but are very confident.	
Dragon	1940, 1952, 1964, 1976, 1988, 2000	The Dragon is associated with the element of Earth and is most compatible with the Rat and the Monkey. The Dragon is prideful and helpful; Dragons are hard working and generous but cannot bear restrictions.	
Snake	1941, 1953, 1965, 1977, 1989, 2001	The Snake is associated with the element of Fire and is most compatible with the Ox and the Rooster. The Snake is self-reliant and introspective; Snakes can be demanding but intuitive.	
Horse	1942, 1954, 1966, 1978, 1990, 2002	The Horse is associated with the element of Fire and is most compatible with the Tiger and the Dog. The Horse is tireless and active; Horses must set their own deadlines and are sometimes quick to judge.	
Goat	1943, 1955, 1967, 1979, 1991, 2003	The Goat is associated with the element of Earth and is most compatible with the Rabbit and the Pig. The Goat is emotional and kind. Goats are polite but shy, and worry too much.	

You're such a	When were you born?	Tell me a little about yourself	Can you send a picture?
Monkey	1944, 1956, 1968, 1980, 1992, 2004	The Monkey is associated with the element of Metal and is most compatible with the Rat and the Dragon. The Monkey is an intelligent problem solver; Monkeys can be oblivious to others and may not understand how their actions affect other people.	
Rooster	1945, 1957, 1969, 1981, 1993, 2005	The Rooster is associated with the element of Metal and is most compatible with the Ox and the Snake. The Rooster is sociable and enjoys being the center of attention; Roosters are strong-willed but can be negative.	
Dog	1946, 1958, 1970, 1982, 1994, 2006	The Dog is associated with the element of Earth and is most compatible with the Tiger and the Horse. The Dog is loyal and dependable. Dogs listen to others but can be critical.	
Pig	1947, 1959, 1971, 1983, 1995, 2007	The Pig is associated with the element of Water and is most compatible with the Rabbit and the Goat. The Pig is honest, kind and friendly. Pigs are popular and dislike conflict; they tend to overindulge.	

Discovering your Compass numbers

Numbers have energy or *chi,* just as everything else does. Every person has his or her own Compass number, sometimes called a *Kua* number. Use this number — which relates to the Magic Square — to help find the most favorable position for you to face when sleeping and making decisions. See Table 1-2. Here you'll see that male and female energies are treated differently in Feng Shui. This goes back to the separation and complimentary aspects of yin and yang energy.

Table 1-2	Discovering Your Compass Numbers	
Sex	**Year Born**	**Compass Number**
Men	1936, 1945, 1954, 1963, 1972, 1981, 1990, 1999, and 2008	1
Women	1932, 1941, 1950, 1959, 1968, 1977, 1986, 1995, and 2004	1
Men	1944, 1953, 1962, 1971, 1980, 1989, 1998, and 2007	2
Women	1933, 1942, 1951, 1960, 1969, 1978, 1987, 1996 and 2005	2
Men	1943, 1952, 1961, 1970, 1979, 1988, 1997, and 2006	3
Women	1934, 1943, 1952, 1961, 1970, 1979, 1988, 1997, and 2006	3
Men	1942, 1951, 1960, 1969, 1978, 1987, 1996, and 2005	4
Women	1935, 1944, 1953, 1962, 1971, 1980, 1989, 1998, and 2007	4
Men	1941, 1950, 1959, 1968, 1977, 1986, 1995, and 2004	5
Women	1936, 1945, 1954, 1963, 1972, 1981, 1990, 1999, and 2008	5
Men	1940, 1949, 1958, 1967, 1976, 1985, 1994, and 2003	6
Women	1937, 1946, 1955, 1964, 1973, 1982, 1991, and 2000	6
Men	1939, 1948, 1957, 1966, 1975, 1984, 1993, and 2002	7
Women	1938, 1947, 1956, 1965, 1974, 1983, 1992, and 2001	7

Sex	Year Born	Compass Number
Men	1938, 1947, 1956, 1965, 1974, 1983, 1992, and 2001	8
Women	1939, 1948, 1957, 1966, 1975, 1984, 1993, and 2002	8
Men	1937, 1946, 1955, 1964, 1973, 1982, 1991, and 2000	9
Women	1940, 1949, 1958, 1967, 1976, 1985, 1994, and 2003	9

By knowing your Compass number, you can determine your most favorable direction (see Table 1-3).

Table 1-3   Determining Your Most Favorable Direction

Number	Favorable Direction
1	North
2	Southwest
3	East
4	Southeast
5	Center
6	Northwest
7	West
8	Northeast
9	South

- The Number 1 is associated with Water.
- The Number 2 is associated with Earth.
- The Number 3 is associated with Thunder.
- The Number 4 is associated with Wind.
- The Number 5 is associated with Earth.
- The Number 6 is associated with Heaven.
- The Number 7 is associated with Lake.

> ✔ The Number 8 is associated with Mountain.
>
> ✔ The Number 9 is associated with Fire.

Depending on your Compass number, you are either a member of the East Group or the West Group. Table 1-4 tells you more.

Table 1-4   Which Side of the Tracks Are You On?

East Group	West Group
1, 3, 4, 9	2, 5, 6, 7, 8
Members of this group have favorable directions of North, East, South, and Southeast.	Members of this group have favorable directions of Southwest, Northwest, West, Northeast, and Center

Black Sect school

The Black Sect Tantric Buddhism (BTB) school (usually called Black Sect and sometimes Black Hat) is a more recent approach that has been refined and developed by Grand Master Professor Thomas Lin Yun, who brought this concept from China to the West over 35 years ago.

I only have Feng Shui eyes for you

Instead of following a prescribed list of steps to turn your workspace into a Feng Shui paradise, develop and fine tune your Feng Shui eyes. When you understand the concepts of Feng Shui design philosophy, you can *see* how these concepts work in different spaces you encounter.

When you walk into a reception area that immediately makes you feel relaxed and at home, you might look around and notice that the space is furnished with natural materials, that the spotless windows allow natural light into the space, and that the area is clean and uncluttered. Your Feng Shui eyes are picking up on the elements that make you feel comfortable.

You can also use your Feng Shui eyes to understand what makes you so uncomfortable about your next-door neighbor's house. Maybe it's the collection of wrought iron gates she has displayed in her living room (too much metal). Maybe it's the way every available surface is crammed with ornaments and knickknacks and you can't make your way to the kitchen without scraping your shins on the pointed corners of a coffee table (interference with the flow of energy through the space).

Black Sect is a practical combination of traditional Feng Shui, Buddhism, Taoism, energy theory, and Western concepts. Black Sect is simpler than Compass School Feng Shui, and seems to work better in the context of Western culture. It relies on the position of the front door, called the *mouth of chi,* and especially emphasizes the occupant's intention. BTB has become very popular in the United States, and it's the method we use in this book. Roll up your sleeves and get started!

Getting in Touch with Your Masculine Side with Yin/Yang

Taoist philosophy, a traditional, mystical Chinese philosophy that teaches how unassertive action and simplicity can create long life and good fortune, says that the universe is made up of opposing yet harmonious elements. These elements are complementary to each other: day and night, dark and light, male and female, yin and yang. You cannot have one without the other.

One of the essential concepts of Feng Shui is *balancing the qualities of yin-yang* that are present in your space. *Yin* is associated with feminine, darkness, rounded shapes, and passive energy. *Yang* is associated with masculine, light, angular shapes, and active energy. Table 1-5 has more yin-yang opposites.

In Feng Shui, the correct balance between yin elements and yang elements should be present. By balancing colors, shapes and textures, you can prevent your space from being out of equilibrium. Too much red paint on the walls equals too much yang; not enough lighting means too much yin. Too much passive yin and you fall asleep at your desk; too much active yang and you can't concentrate on the report you're writing.

You can often tell a space has too much yin or too much yang by how uncomfortable you feel after a while. Feeling dispirited and depressed, or feeling groggy and ready for an afternoon nap probably indicates too many yin elements; feeling high strung, distracted, and even angry can mean too many yang elements. Remember with good Feng Shui, *it's all in the balance!* Chapter 3 can help you achieve that balance. Chapter 4 tells you what you need to know about color, texture, and lighting. Oh, and plants, too.

Table 1-5	Yin/Yang Opposites
Yin	*Yang*
Earth	Heaven
Moon	Sun
Feminine	Masculine
Cold	Hot
Dark	Light
Night	Day
Soft	Hard
Passive	Active
Round	Angular
Quiet	Loud

Flowing Like Chi

Feng Shui relies on the concept of *chi,* or energy. Feng Shui teaches that chi is the life force that flows through the universe, and is present in all living things; it permeates the land and sky as well as people.

In the same way, chi flows through our spaces. If chi is blocked, a depressed energy level may result and we may be uncomfortable in our surroundings. Freely moving chi makes us feel good. When you walk into a space where the chi flows freely, you may think, "This is a good atmosphere. This is a happy place."

To imagine how chi flows, think of it as a flowing river. Could water move freely and gently through your space? If, in your workspace, a current of water would get stuck in cluttered corners (like an eddy in a stream eventually becoming stagnant and filled with debris) you probably need to make some changes and remove the clutter to unblock the chi. Chapter 2 talks about getting chi where it needs to be: Ban the clutter!

High Five-ing Elements

Feng Shui teaches that everything is made up of Five Elements. These elements are Earth, Metal, Water, Wood, and Fire. Each of the elements has its yin (passive) side and its yang (active) side. Think of water. In a placid lake, water is calm and tranquil. Now think of a storm at sea, with the water pounding against the shore — this is water that can erode a cliff. Ideally, we want to surround ourselves in our office or home with *balanced* elemental energy.

When selecting materials to use in your space, take into consideration how they represent the five elements, as shown in Table 1-6. A wooden floor is more inviting than a vinyl floor. Wicker, wood, and cotton fabrics are all comfortable and attractive. Natural lighting is better and more restful for our eyes than artificial lighting, and natural objects, such as plants and flowers, raise our spirits and our chi! Chapter 2 helps you raise chi and Chapter 4 explains textures, lighting, and plants.

Table 1-6	Elements and Their Materials
Element	*Associated Materials*
Bamboo and wicker	Wood
Natural fabrics (cotton and linen, for example)	Wood
Lighting (natural or artificial)	Fire
Glass and mirrors	Water
Metal furniture, picture frames, light fixtures	Metal
Clay, terra cotta, and ceramic	Earth
Stone, granite, and marble	Earth

Heed this warning, though: Too much emphasis on one element has its drawbacks.

- ✔ Water helps you feel renewed, but too much can make you feel like you're drowning or wishy-washy in decision making.

- ✔ Wood enhances flexibility, but too much is associated with extreme idealism (not very businesslike).

✔ Fire invigorates, but too much can over stimulate you.

✔ Earth supports you, but too much is associated with being overly cautious and fearful of risks.

✔ Metal makes you feel strong, but too much is associated with aggression or being unwilling to compromise.

Going with the Octagon

Each direction and area of your office has a different type of energy associated with it. An eight-sided figure, called the *Bagua* (ba-gwa) symbolizes the different energies of the directions.

The Bagua (also called the *Pakua* or *Feng Shui Octagon*) shown in Figure 3-2 (in Chapter 3) shows each direction's quality. The center is associated overall health and well being and corresponds with the number 5.

✔ The outer edge shows the sector, or *gua*.

✔ The next row shows the element.

✔ The element's shape is next.

✔ The color associated with each sector is innermost.

Chapter 2

Moving and Grooving with Chi

*C*hi may be called *life energy* or *life force.* Present in all living things, it flows through the universe, created by and affecting the land and sky as well as people. In your body, chi flows along meridians or channels; if these channels are blocked, ill health can result. You may feel you lack energy. Just as chi flows through your body, it flows through your environment. If chi is *blocked,* or not allowed to flow freely, it may become stagnant, depressing the energy in your environment and perhaps making you feel uncomfortable in your surroundings. Freely moving chi makes you feel energetic and positive.

In this chapter, we show you how to establish the free flow of chi in your workspace, including clearing pathways and keeping your space clutter-free. We'll give you tips for fixing common chi problems, including unfavorable floor plans. In Feng Shui parlance, these tips for fixing chi problems are called *cures.*

Opening Wide to See the Mouth of Chi

Everything that comes into your workspace enters through your front door, bringing its positive and negative energy with it. In Feng Shui, the front entrance is called the *Mouth of Chi*. This might be the front door of the store where you work as a clerk, the door to your office, or the opening to your cubicle. The Mouth of Chi is one of the most important and powerful areas in your workspace. It is through the Mouth of Chi that good fortune, blessings, and opportunities come to you. Do your best to welcome them in! Making a good first impression is how you can start.

Creating a negative first impression — dirty windows near the entrance and unemptied trashcans by the front door — may cause chi to stagnate and may even attract negative chi. If nothing else, it will turn off potential clients!

The Mouth of Chi also allows people to enter. What these other people see when they enter your space is a reflection of who you are. Think of the Mouth of Chi as a mirror of your personality. Is the entrance to your workspace inviting or disorderly? Cluttered or easy to navigate? The image you project and the impression others have of your space affects the energy coming into your space, whether that impression is favorable or unfavorable.

Remember that your workspace entrance will leave a lasting impression on clients, visitors, and co-workers. Make sure it's the impression you want them to have. Your retail store's front door should be easily accessible (you shouldn't have to navigate sixteen steeply pitched steps to reach it), well lit, clean, and welcoming (get rid of the sign saying, "Attack dog in back"). Even the entrance to your cubicle reflects well on you if you take the time to keep the area free of clutter and position your desk and other equipment appropriately. If you meet clients at your office building, both the building's main entrance and your workspace entrance should be clean and clutter-free. This will make your clients more comfortable doing business with you.

Convincing your boss to keep the front entrance to your place of work clean and inviting can be a challenge. If she isn't open to Feng Shui, use words like *welcoming* and *comfortable* to convince her that paying attention to the entrance will enhance the bottom line. In fact, you can even spend a few minutes before or after work sprucing up the area to show your boss what a difference a little attention can make. Or show her Chapter 7 of this book, which is just for CEOs. If all else fails and she's not open to your suggestions, focus on those areas over which you do have control.

Sometimes the placement of the entrance to your workspace is awkward or inconvenient. Maybe the door to your space opens onto a wall or visitors have to come to it from a less favorable direction. Moving the door is probably not an option, but you can help correct this problem by making the entrance more inviting. Here are a few tips on how to do just that:

 ✔ **Clean and de-clutter the entrance area** and *keep* it clean and uncluttered. Sweep or vacuum the floor near the entrance. Signs of neglect make visitors feel uncomfortable. More on removing clutter in this chapter's "Bustin' Clutter to Break Chi Free" section.

 ✔ **For exterior entrances, keep the door freshly painted.** Dark or bright colors, like red or navy blue, and natural wood make good colors for front doors.

 ✔ **Windows near a front entrance should be kept scrupulously clean.**

 ✔ **Healthy plants or blooming plants in colored bowls placed by a front door** or near the entrance make a space feel attractive. Avoid cactus and spiked-leafed plants, which can make visitors feel unwelcome.

 ✔ **Make sure the area is well lit and that lamps are hanging straight.** Add a floor lamp or indirect lighting if needed. Chapter 4 talks more about lighting.

 ✔ **Hang a Feng Shui mirror** (an octagon-shaped mirror, called a *Bagua mirror*) above the front entrance on the outside of the building to deflect negative chi from the entrance. See Chapter 3 for more information.

 ✔ **A circular or oval-shaped welcome mat** for exterior entrances counteracts the rectangular shape of the door and doorway, and subtly makes the area feel more balanced and harmonious.

 ✔ **Add a water feature such as a tabletop fountain or desktop waterfall** near the entryway to make guests (and you!) feel welcome. Gently moving water has a calming effect on people. See Chapter 4 for further information.

> ✔ **Position a pair of symbolically protective figures on either side of your entrance.** Instead of the lions that "guard" many structures, think of colorful flowers or small stone or ceramic figures of angels or other protective figures.

Don't place decorative objects too close to or directly in front of the entrance to your office. Not only can this feel unwelcoming to visitors, it can also block the good chi from entering your space. See Figure 2-1 for what turns out a really poor first impression. The front door is set back from the front wall, creating a dark, unwelcoming hall. The wind has blown leaves and debris into the areaway. The entrance is not welcoming. The trash has not been picked up. See Figure 2-2 for examples on how to make a better first impression. Plants and a water feature would enhance this entrance; but at least the trash is picked up, the entrance is easily accessible and the windows are clean!

Figure 2-1: This first impression? Not so good.

Figure 2-2: This one? Much better, but still not perfect.

Constructing Fabulous Floor Plans

So you're in the door. The way your workspace is arranged, from the placement of the front door to the position of your desk, affects the movement of chi throughout your space. If your desk is in a less favorable position, that's pretty easy to fix — just move your desk. What if your office door faces the wrong direction? That's not so easy to cure. (Your boss might object to moving the door to the opposite wall.)

When we talk about *floor plans,* we're essentially talking about your space's architectural details: the shape of your office, the placement of the door and windows, columns. When we talk about *layouts,* we mean the way furniture and other moveable objects have been placed in the room.

Unfortunately, architects and builders don't always take Feng Shui into consideration when they create buildings with hard-to-find or irregularly placed doorways (*not* auspicious or favorable) or when they locate the toilet in the Wealth sector (bye-bye profits). So often, we are left with less-than-ideal floor plans where we work. But Feng Shui is about finding solutions, and solutions don't have to include tearing out walls.

The placement of objects, such as desks and chairs, is crucial to the free flow of chi. Poor furniture arrangement can cancel out the benefits of an auspicious floor plan, just as placing furniture correctly can help counteract the effects of a poor floor plan. See Chapters 8 through 13 for more specifics on arranging furniture in different types of workspaces.

What's in a floor plan?

In Chapter 1 we talk about the Nine Life Sectors in the Bagua, the eight-sided figure that symbolizes the different energies of the directions. We show how the Bagua corresponds to your workspace. Knowing this helps you figure out the most favorable locations for different furnishings. In the same way, you can use the Bagua for an entire office building, factory, or hardware store to favorably place various departments or objects. Putting the cash register in the Wealth sector is a good start!

If a section of the Bagua is missing, that could cause problems for the business and a cure is needed. If your Wealth Sector is missing, you may find yourself in bankruptcy court faster than you thought possible. You can symbolically complete the missing sector by adding cures such as lights, flags, and mirrors. See Chapter 16 for more information about cures.

Staking claim: The best spot for you

The farther your workspace is from the front door, the more positive energy your space has. Power accumulates in the back of a building, and it's also quieter, with less traffic.

CEOs ideally are in the ultimate command position — farthest from the door, facing it, and energetically protected by the workers in the front of the office. However, if you're the CEO, don't make the mistake of claiming the penthouse suite for your office. Being too high up in a building can make you feel unprotected and less grounded; besides, being closer to the ground floor will help you get out of a building faster in case of an emergency.

Although the main entrance is the most important to consider, most buildings have other entrances and it is favorable to position your space away from those entrances. If you're on a floor above the ground floor, elevators and staircases are similar to entrances. They can cause chi to rush away from your space. Position your workspace away from these entrances as well.

Your best position in the building depends on what you do. The following types of jobs are best done in the sectors listed:

- ✔ **Accountants, bookkeepers, and other financial people** should be located in the southeastern sector: the Wealth sector.

- ✔ **Creative people** should be located in the western sector: the Children/Creativity sector.

- ✔ **Human resources** workers should be located in the southwestern sector: the Relationship sector.

- ✔ **Managers** should be located in the northwestern sector: the Helpful People sector.

- ✔ **Researchers** should be located in the northeastern sector: the Knowledge sector.

Shaping up

The ideal workspace is a square or rectangle with windows that let in natural light. The regular shape means all parts of the Bagua are present and accounted for. The entrance should face your favorable direction (an entrance that faces south is usually auspicious). See Chapter 1 to determine your most favorable direction.

If the view from your office window is blocked by a tall building or wall, your career can energetically suffer. Mentally and emotionally, you feel blocked and depressed. The same is true if the window is stuck, doesn't move, or is broken. Workspaces that are oddly or irregularly shaped are not favorable, because when you overlay the Bagua on them, parts of the space may be missing, or parts of the space may project beyond the boundaries of the Bagua. Irregularly shaped rooms also make it difficult for the chi to move freely and smoothly throughout the space. L-shaped, T-shaped and U-shaped workspaces are also not favorable. See Figure 2-3 for an example of a good floor plan, with all the Life Sectors in place; see Figure 2-4 for examples of poor floor plans, with missing Life Sectors. Turn to the Appendix to find some blank floor plans you can use to sketch your own workspace

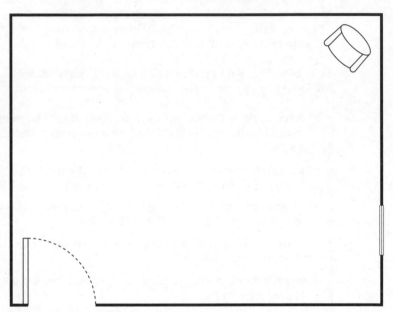

Figure 2-3: Being a square was never cool before. The room has all nine Life Sectors and the window lets in natural light.

Keep these tips in mind when working on your floor plan:

✔ Sitting with your back to a window can make you feel vulnerable and unsupported.

✔ Take down any object that hangs over your chair. Hanging objects such as plants, mobiles, and light fixtures can feel threatening.

✔ Move your chair so that you don't sit directly under beams.

✔ In a work area with more than one desk or an office with several pieces of large furniture, arrange furnishings in semicircular patterns. They ideally face the entrance.

✔ If two people share a space, position each work area/desk to give some privacy and the ability to focus. Desks directly facing each other can be distracting.

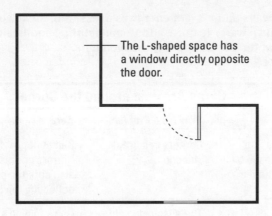

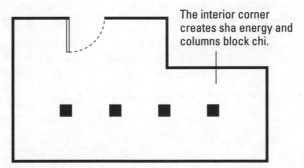

Figure 2-4: Poor floor plans show irregularly shaped rooms.

Fixing a funky floor plan

To understand the importance of curing unfavorable floor plans, it's helpful to know why the layout is unfavorable. Table 2-1 lists some common floor plan challenges and explains why they are problematic. Table 2-1 also offers some solutions for these challenging layouts. (Getting a new job is not the sort of solution we have in mind!) The challenges identified here are just a sample of the ones you may encounter. Any Feng Shui cure will help balance a problem floor plan. See Chapter 16 for more information on cures.

If you're not sure how to fix a problem, try one cure at a time. If it works, great. If not, try a different cure. You can add more than one cure to your space. Don't expect overnight problem solving. Try a cure and give it a few weeks before you give up on it. Experimenting is perfectly fine — and perfectly fun!

You can always add vibrant energy to a less-than-ideal workspace by including a water feature, additional lighting, and healthy plants. Chapter 4 talks about these elements.

Table 2-1	Cures Are Just around the Corner	
Problem	*Why It's a Problem*	*Cure*
Corners face into the room caused by irregularly shaped walls	Corners can create sha chi.	Camouflage with plants. Mirrors or crystals can also cure the problem by deflecting the cutting chi.
Entrance faces a large window or another door	The auspicious chi can leave the room.	Use a folding screen to block escaping chi.
Workspace entrance at the end of a long, narrow hallway	Subject to arrows of sha chi, negative energy.	Add a crystal or wind chime to your doorway to defuse the cutting chi.
Heavy beams, soffits, and duct work	Causes heavy chi and can feel threatening and uncomfortable.	Cover with false or drop ceilings, or paint a lighter color. Or, hang a crystal from the ceiling. Don't place desks or chairs directly underneath the beams.
Glass walls	Can make you feel vulnerable and unsupported.	Cover with blinds or shades or hang crystals in front of them. Balance glass (which represents Water) with Earth (marble, granite) or Fire (red accents). See Chapter 1 for more information about the Five Elements.
Irregularly shaped floor plans	One or more Life Sectors are missing. This can have unfortunate effects on your career. If your Wealth sector is missing, you may find it harder to get a raise or meet your sales goals.	Place a crystal or mirror to energetically complete the missing area; place a screen-type room divider across an L- or T-shaped area to symbolically create a square or rectangle out of the rest of the workspace.

Problem	Why It's a Problem	Cure
Long, narrow office	Chi may rush through the space instead of flowing gently and freely.	Can be shortened by adding a screen, modular room divider, armoire, or other large piece of furniture across one of the short walls.
Posts, pillars, and columns	Blocks the flow of chi and may send cutting, negative chi toward you.	Round columns are not as bad as square ones. Columns and posts can be softened using plants or mirrors.
Door in full view of a bathroom	Flushes away the beneficial chi instead of allowing it to move freely about.	Keep the bathroom door closed. Add a mirror to the back of the bathroom door to reflect the chi back into the workspace.

Taking the Ouch from Angles

Sha chi, or *killing breath,* is a negative arrow of cutting energy that creates discomfort and seems subtly threatening. Visualize someone pointing a finger at you and saying, "No, no, no!" It wouldn't feel so good. That's what a sha arrow is like. When such negative chi arrows are directed at a dwelling or occur within a space, they bring a high level of energetic discomfort.

Feng Shui is about feelings. Energetic discomfort feels unsettling, ungrounded, and even threatening. In a work environment, negative sha arrows can produce stress or discomfort. Workers in such a space may be less productive and more irritable.

Positive chi doesn't travel in an arrow. It meanders like a gentle stream or brook. The energy of positive chi is tranquil and gentle. Being in an environment of positive chi helps a worker feel more serene and comfortable. People who feel this way are more likely to be productive, positive, and pleasant to other workers.

Sha chi is produced by strong winds, sharp corners in adjacent or nearby buildings, peaked rooflines, power lines, telephone poles, or high energy transformers. A Feng Shui mirror placed outside the building, above the front door can deflect these bad arrows of energy. These traditional Bagua mirrors are only used outside a building. If a Bagua mirror isn't available, any reflective surface resembling a mirror can be effective in deflecting negative chi from an outside source. One of Holly's more creative clients used a shiny, half-moon–shaped hubcap! Other cures, such as a water feature can also deflect the negative chi from entering the building.

But the outside world isn't the only place you'll find sha chi. Inside your workspace, sharp corners from inside walls, edges on tables and picture frames, and any sharp or pointed design element all create sha arrows. Sharp corners are like energetic fingers constantly poking at you, making you feel uneasy. A few edges are fine, and edges that don't point directly at you as you're working are generally more neutral than those that stab towards you.

Choose office furnishings with rounded corners and without sharp, pointy corners or edges. Table 2-2 gives you an idea of what you need.

Table 2-2 Common Problems with Office Furnishings

Problem	Solution
Angular furniture	A cotton afghan (or other natural fiber) placed on a piece of furniture can hide some of its corners. Afghans don't have to be used only on sofas. The same is true of throw pillows, which soften hard edges.
Sharp angles on windows	Soft window coverings.
Plants with spiky leaves create symbolic arrows in your environment	Plants with round or oval-shaped leaves. (See more about selecting plants and flowers in Chapter 4.)
A bookcase tends to be made up of all angles and corners	Add a fern or a flowering plant to camouflage at least a few of the angles. OR Glass fronted bookcases or armoires with doors instead of open shelves.
Sharp cornered picture frames to hold your diplomas and awards	Picture frames with rounded corners.

But even if you can't sell all your office furnishings and start over, you don't have to suffer the consequences of sha chi. Feng Shui provides cures for almost any energy problem.

Possible cures for the negative sha arrows that corners and angles produce include:

- **Crystals:** Especially faceted crystal spheres. You can place a crystal on a surface or hang it in front of the sharp edge. When hanging a Feng Shui cure like a crystal, use a red string or ribbon. The color red is very powerful, as it is the most yang color and symbolizes fire and positive change. Crystals can be purchased at gift shops and New Age stores.

- **Mirrors:** Preferably in a circular or Bagua-shaped (octagonal) frame. A mirror placed above your desk will show you who walks into your space, especially important if your back is to the entrance.

- **Healthy plants:** Their greenery can camouflage pointed corners and edges.

- **Wind chimes:** Be polite and don't use chimes if you share a workspace with others.

Going with the Pathway's Flow

Once the chi enters your space through the Mouth of Chi, it must continue to circulate gently to bring good energy throughout the space. For example, if the hallway outside your office door is constantly crowded with boxes, trashcans, and unclaimed umbrellas, the good energy gets trapped and prevented from going forward, and in all likelihood so do you! Chi that gets stuck or splintered depresses the energy level in your workspace and can make a working environment feel stagnant and tired.

In addition to softening corners and hiding angles, consider ways to Feng Shui the pathways in your space. If people can't move freely from one place to another, you can be sure the chi doesn't flow freely either.

The easiest way to keep chi from getting blocked in your space is to move objects out of the way. Keeping places clear of clutter helps keep the chi moving. But not so fast there, partner: Subtleties exist.

Good chi gone bad

It sounds like clean hallways are all you need to fix your chi; after that everything will be fine, right? Unfortunately, straight and direct pathways can be a problem. Such pathways funnel the chi too quickly through your space. This creates *sha chi,* or negative, cutting energy.

Curved pathways slow chi. Wider and shorter hallways allow chi to move more slowly through the space; long, narrow hallways require the most attention. However, because builders love to build at right angles and buildings these days are getting bigger, chances are the hallways in your workspace are all perfectly straight. No gentle curves here: just 90-degree angles.

That's not the only problem. Sometimes older buildings or buildings that have been remodeled in a less-than-Feng-Shui way have long, narrow rooms that cause chi to rush through them at a breakneck pace. Some cures to slow down chi:

- ✔ Good **lighting** (hanging lights are most effective).
- ✔ **Mirrors** placed alternately along opposite walls.
- ✔ **Patterned** rugs and **textured** walls.
- ✔ Potted **plants** in round containers.

Doors in a hallway should be regularly spaced across from each other, and not directly in front of each other. If doors are unevenly spaced, they're called *biting doors.* Hanging a crystal opposite biting doors balances their energy.

Seeing all pathways

Hallways are not the only pathways in your workspace. The pathways that move traffic throughout your workspace — from your desk to the file cabinet, for instance — are just as important as the walkway that leads to the front door of the office building.

If these pathways are cluttered or difficult to navigate (perhaps they're very narrow or you can't get through when someone is using the file cabinet) not only does it block chi, but also it causes frustration. Every time you stub your toe on the box of office supplies that really needs to be put in the office supply cabinet, you're causing negative emotions and low-level annoyance that can build to high levels of stress.

Here's how to remedy this problem:

1. **Identify the important pathways in your workspace.**

   You can do this easily by considering the important pieces of equipment you use and the places you commonly go.

2. **Ask yourself if you can move freely from one place to another.**

   Do you constantly have to move your co-worker's chair out of the way to get to the coffeepot?

3. **Consider how to clear these pathways.**

   Make certain that the traffic patterns in and around your workspace are clear and uncluttered.

   If possible, arrange furniture so that the pathways curve gently rather than move directly from one point to another.

Bustin' Clutter to Break Chi Free

Our workspaces quickly fill up with equipment, paper, files, computer disks, references books and piles of objects that we feel we must have to function. But those piles of reports stacked on your floor cause stagnation and frustration. They represent blocked chi. All of this stuck energy makes you feel depressed and weighs down visitors and co-workers, too. By banishing clutter from your workspace, you'll feel more energetic and the chi within the office will move more freely.

Getting rid of clutter is the single most important thing you can do to Feng Shui your workspace. But what is clutter, exactly? Clutter can take many forms: overflowing wastebaskets, dying plants (which represent dead or dying chi), dust piled on your computer monitor. Figure 2-5 shows clutter as its worst.

Identifying clutter

"But that's not clutter!" you say. "That's the annual report from 1966, and someday I just might have to refer to it!" As hard as it is for us to part with our much-loved personal belongings when it's time to clean up our houses, it's often harder for us to part with our clutter in our workspaces.

Sometimes we don't feel like we have the authority to get rid of the clutter — if we throw out that annual report from 1966 and it turns out someone does need it, it won't do our careers any good. We also sometimes don't like to take responsibility for the clutter. We're not the only ones who use the supply closet; why should we be the ones to go through it and discard all those dried-up bottles of liquid paper? But enough with the excuses! Take a look around you with a detached mindset. What do you actually see?

Figure 2-5: Clutter creates chaos, and who needs more of that?

Kicking clutter in the bum

Your goal is to pare down and simplify. Order and simplicity are the bywords of Feng Shui. Repeat after us: reduce and recycle, reduce and recycle . . .

Although you can do this one desk drawer at a time, the most effective (although drastic) approach is to remove everything and then put back only what you absolutely, positively must have. (And you should have a very strict interpretation of what *must-have* means. Usually, must-have means those items you use on a daily basis. All other items can be trashed, donated, or stored elsewhere.)

Since this may be an overwhelming process, you might want to come in on a Saturday morning to do it. The following list helps you on your journey to a cleaner desk:

1. **Decide what *must-have* means to you.**

2. **Collect some boxes to dump your stuff in while you sort.**

3. **Remove everything from the top of your desk and dump everything out of your drawers.**

4. **Give your desk a nice cleaning.**

   Get all those potato chip crumbs out of your bottom drawer and wipe up that sticky spot in your center drawer.

5. **Put only the bare necessities on top of your desk.**

   This may include your phone, your computer, a pen, and a pad of paper (or whatever is appropriate for your work).

   Get rid of the fuzzy dice and the posable figure from McDonald's and the tape dispenser in the shape of a golf club that doesn't dispense tape. Keep only things you absolutely love which are also functional.

6. **Put back into your desk drawers only those things you use at least once a week.**

   Everything else can go somewhere else like the recycle bin or the thrift store. Recycle those mounds of paper. Not even the IRS expects you to save your receipts forever.

7. **Go on to the next areas — the storage room, the file cabinet, the credenza — and give them the same treatment.**

   Don't be surprised at how much trash you generate — get rid of it. Figure 2-6 shows busted clutter.

 At the very least, move the clutter out of your immediate workspace and give it a new home. Box it up and have it stored somewhere out of sight on the premises if you're reluctant to simply throw it away.

 Once you've cleared the clutter, you have to keep it cleared. That's actually the hard part. If you're not careful, all that clutter will be back in about two weeks. Controlling it starts with understanding what causes it. Ask yourself if you

✔ **Generate a lot of paper.**

✔ **Tend to leave things where you last use them.**

✔ **Have to walk halfway across the building to file something you use everyday.**

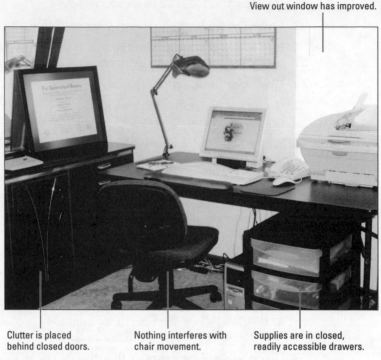

View out window has improved.

Clutter is placed behind closed doors.

Nothing interferes with chair movement.

Supplies are in closed, readily accessible drawers.

Figure 2-6: Squeaky clean. Know what we mean?

Now create a plan for keeping clutter under control.

- ✔ **Create a filing system.**
- ✔ **Designate an area of your workspace (desktop, drawers, and so on) for items.**
- ✔ **Take five minutes to put things back where they go.** Do this at the end of the day, even if you have to retrieve them the very next day.

Enlisting the troops

Your workspace probably exists in proximity to other people's workspaces. You probably share a bathroom with fellow workers, a copy room with the other people on the fourth floor, and a board room with the entire staff. Although you can keep your little corner of the world clutter free if you set your mind to it, what about the rest of the space?

Feeling trashy

If it's not convenient to throw unusable items away, you'll probably put off doing it. Keep trashcans conveniently located in your workspace and out of sight if possible. It's not overkill to have a trashcan near your drafting table and another one near your desk. Keeping trash sitting around is visually unappealing, can cause stuck chi, and may even invite negative chi (not to mention negative comments) into your workspace.

They should be

✔ Covered so that you don't have to see the contents.

✔ Big enough to do the job.

✔ Emptied frequently.

And you don't have to send everything to the landfill. Recycling is good Feng Shui, which is based on honoring the earth and respecting natural resources. From ancient times its teachings have advocated the idea of treading lightly on the planet and promoting the beauty of nature. Feng Shui was then and is still now a strong proponent of recycling and the wise use of natural resources. The term *sustainable living* fits perfectly into the idea of good Feng Shui.

Encourage other co-workers, especially office or cubicle-mates, to join you in your battle against clutter with these steps:

1. **Set a good example.**

   Keep your own area neat and tidy. If someone leaves her Styrofoam coffee cup on your desk, show her where it can be recycled.

2. **Outline the benefits of keeping the place in order.**

   If your co-workers won't buy into Feng Shui, accept that some people just don't care to participate. Or take a lighter approach, and instead of lecturing your co-workers on the importance of free-flowing chi, joke about having to move six boxes of envelopes out of the way to reach the copy machine.

3. **Take responsibility.**

   You can pick up the litter cluttering the entryway to the building. You can talk to your boss about encouraging other employees to do their part. You can spearhead a recycling campaign. You can take control.

Cleaning up your company's act

Encourage your boss (or do this yourself if you are the boss) to sponsor a clean-up day (or afternoon or hour). All employees will spend the time cleaning up and de-cluttering the office. With everyone pitching in, the job will go faster, no one will feel resentful, and you can ask someone else if they think you'll ever need that annual report from 1966. Wear old clothes, order in pizza, and make it a fun time. If your boss balks, explain how de-cluttering the place will improve productivity and therefore enhance the bottom line. That should get her attention!

Chapter 3

Gathering People and Principles Together

●●

In This Chapter
▶ Putting it all together
▶ Evaluating your workspace
▶ Solving Feng Shui problems

●●

You can rattle off the Five Elements and the definition of chi, and you're ready to implement the principles of Feng Shui in your workspace. Well, you're almost ready for action . . . we say *almost* because you have to understand how the various principles of Feng Shui interact with each other; they don't exist in isolation. You also have to consider how your use of Feng Shui has an impact on other people.

In this chapter we give you the low-down on connecting the Bagua to the Five Elements and provide tips for talking others into keeping their minds open about Feng Shui.

Combining the Five Elements

To keep the energy of your space in equilibrium, ensure a balanced representation of all Five Elements: Earth, Metal, Water, Wood, and Fire. If all of the elements exist in a space and none of the elements dominates, you get a feeling of comfort and harmony.

The elements are sometimes represented symbolically. The color red, for instance, is symbolic of fire. And certain shapes represent each element. See Figure 3-1 for a drawing of the Five Elements.

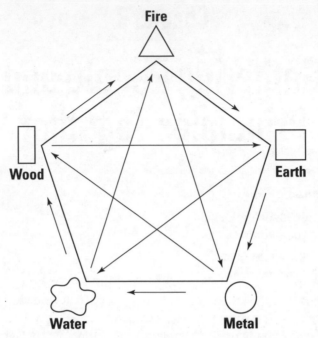

Figure 3-1: Come on baby, light my Fire: The Five Elements and their shape symbols.

Understanding the Five Elements and how they work together is basic to understanding Feng Shui. The Five Elements are Fire, Earth, Metal, Water, and Wood. Taken in this order, they form the Nourishing Cycle in which Fire creates Earth (ashes), Earth generates Metal (ore), Metal holds Water (container), and Water nourishes Wood (plant life).

In order to bring elemental balance into an environment, one of the goals is to have all Five Elements represented; literally, by using wood furniture, or symbolically, as when you have a representation of each element present within a space. In doing so, the occupants or workers will have a heightened sense of tranquility and well-being, thus furthering the idea of greater productivity in the work place and a higher degree of job satisfaction. Not bad!

Nourishing:

> WOOD feeds FIRE
>
> FIRE makes EARTH
>
> EARTH creates METAL

METAL holds WATER

WATER nurtures WOOD

When there is an imbalance or a greater amount of one element over another, using the Controlling Cycle of the Elements will help bring design elements within the work place back into balance.

Controlling:

WOOD consumes EARTH

EARTH blocks WATER

WATER extinguishes FIRE

FIRE melts METAL

METAL cuts WOOD

The two cycles work in conjunction with each other; one is not better than the other. Both cycles are powerful ways to enhance the energy within a space. For this reason, if you need to enhance your Career sector, add a Water cure. This could be a water feature, such as a Feng Shui fountain, a small aquarium, a mirror, or a crystal. And remember that Water is symbolized by using the color black or dark blue, so objects in these hues act as enhancers.

Table 3-1 explains how each element is represented by a specific color, a direction, certain types of objects, and mental and emotional aspects of life.

Table 3-1	Elements and Their Characteristics
Element	*Characteristics*
Wood	•Greens and blues
	•Plants and flowers, all wood
	•East
	•Intuition and inspiration
Fire	•Reds
	•Lighting, candles, fireplace, sunlight
	•South
	•Emotion and passion

(continued)

Table 3-1 *(continued)*

Element	Characteristics
Earth	•Yellows and earth tones
	•Soil, ceramics, tile, brick, stucco
	•Grounded and loyal
	•Southwest and Northeast
Metal	•White and pastel colors
	•Rock and stone, all metal
	•West
	•Focus and mental acuity
Water	•Black and dark colors
	•Water features, glass, crystal, mirrors
	•North
	•Spiritual

Table 3-2 shows you how to enhance a particular characteristic by using its associated element.

Table 3-2   **Want to Make Some Changes?**

What you want to do	How You Can Get It Done
Encourage the growth of your career.	Add Water to the Career sector.
Improve your reputation or increase your power.	Add Fire to the Fame sector.
Cope with pressures and rapid changes.	Add Earth to the Health sector.
Facilitate communication with others.	Add Metal to the Children/Creativity sector.
Increase your wealth.	Add moving Water (a water feature or a picture of moving water) to the Wealth sector.
Enhance your wisdom and judgment.	Add Earth to the Knowledge area.

Using a 9-to-5 Bagua

Each Bagua sector is connected with what ancient Feng Shui masters considered an important aspect of our lives. The eight outer sectors and the inner circle of the Bagua together total nine Life Sectors. Often the central area is referred to as a home's or office's *T'ai Chi* or *energetic hub*. You can see this in Figure 3-2. The doors at the bottom show the entrance to your workspace, the *Mouth of Chi*. So the main entrance to your office or workspace always falls within one of the three lower sectors: Knowledge, Career, or Helpful People.

The Bagua asserts that the center is the place of our overall health and well being. The other eight sectors are equally important and balanced in the Bagua. None of these eight sectors is given more emphasis than another. The *T'ai Chi* is the culmination or end result of balancing all the other eight Life Sectors. When all the Life Sectors are in balance, the result is overall well being . . . the *T'ai Chi*.

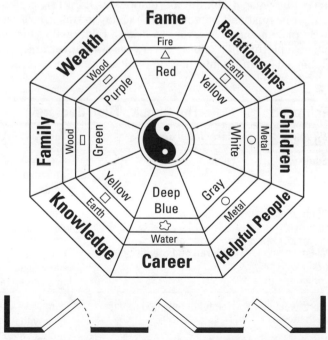

Figure 3-2: The Bagua gives you more bang for your spiritual buck.

Each sector of the Bagua has a corresponding location in your environment. To make changes in a certain area of your life, arrange your space to emphasize the corresponding sector, or *raise that sector's chi.* Consider the Bagua an energetic template for your space. When you place an imaginary Bagua over your workspace, it becomes clear how to place objects to enhance certain Life Sectors.

If you want to enhance your wealth, for instance, place a dish with coins along with a healthy plant on a table in the southeast part (the Wealth sector) of your office. This is also an excellent area for a tabletop fountain, as Water feeds Wood. Also, see Chapter 16 for more about Feng Shui cures.

The south-facing sector of the Bagua is the recognition, exposure, and fame sector. If you're looking for recognition and fame, you can enhance the chi of this area with the Fire Element: Candles, the color red, design elements with triangular shapes, and healthy plant life. (Wood feeds Fire!)

The southwest sector is the relationship sector and has to do with love, marriage, and intimate relationships. Putting a picture of you and your husband on your wedding day in this sector would be a wise placement. If you want to bring a relationship into your life, place a picture of a couple . . . always two, never one or three! See Table 3-3 for more information on directions and sectors.

Table 3-3	The Bagua's Nine Sectors	
Direction	*Associated Sector*	*Workspace Application*
South	Fame	To improve your reputation at work and with clients
Southwest	Marriage	To improve relationships with your co-workers
West	Children and creativity	To improve creative problem-solving and performing creative tasks
Northwest	Helpful people and travel	To improve your relationships with those people who can help your career, such as clients and bosses

Direction	Associated Sector	Workspace Application
North	Career	To improve your career prospects and help you meet your career goals
Northeast	Knowledge and spirituality	To improve your job skills and increase your education with a direct impact on your career
East	Family and elders	To improve your relationships with others, particularly your superiors, and to create a work-life balance
Southeast	Wealth	To improve your career success, increase your wealth, and bring overall abundance into your life
Center	Health and overall well-being	To improve your overall well-being and enjoyment of your work

If a sector is missing in your workspace, then you may have a corresponding problem in your working life. If your career sector is missing, look out: You may soon be transitioning to a new career. If your space has a *projection,* extra chi is circulating in that sector. (And that's good: Think of extra chi within a space as an opportunity for additional abundance and auspicious energy.) If your workspace has a projection in the knowledge sector, don't be surprised if your boss sends you back to school!

How can you tell whether there's extra chi in a space? If a portion of the workspace projects less than half of the length of the wall, this creates a *projection* (an area that provides an opportunity for additional chi).

1. **Determine if your workspace is a regular rectangle or a square.**

2. **If any portion of the four walls juts out less than ½ the distance of the length of that wall, this creates a projection.**

   Chapter 7 has a figure that shows you what a projection looks like.

How can you tell whether a section is missing?

1. **Create a layout of your workspace.**

   Sketch your desktop if you've no office or cubicle.

   This can be a sketch on the back of an old memo with the crayon your kid abandoned in your purse or it can be a sophisticated, detailed plan you create on your computer with special software. Or flip to the Appendix, where we've provided some blank floor plans you can use for your sketch.

2. **Note details such as windows and doors and the placement of architectural features, like columns and posts.**

3. **Determine where the main entrance is located.**

   This primary door will fall within either the Knowledge, Career, or Helpful People sectors. Once this entrance quadrant is determined, the rest of the Bagua falls into place.

4. **Place the Bagua over the room sketch.**

   You can stretch out or squeeze the Bagua to make it cover the layout. Such flexibility is shown in Figure 3-3. The first three show it molded to rooms of different shapes; the last one shows how you fit it over an L-shaped room.

Once you've done this, you can see where the different Life Sectors are in your workspace. If one of them is missing, you can cure it. Or you can raise the chi in a sector (or more than one sector) if you want to achieve a goal related to that sector.

For example, Holly had a commercial Feng Shui client whose office was completely missing its wealth sector. Bills were piling up and customers weren't paying invoices. To cure this missing area and restore the chi that was being lost, Holly symbolically completed the area where the Wealth area would have been by placing a statue at the point outside where the walls would have intersected. An outside spotlight was positioned to shine directly on the statue, further enhancing the chi. An intention was set by the client that by placing this grounding object where the Wealth sector would have been, the business's wealth would be brought back into the building and abundance would be restored to the company. Within several months clients were promptly paying their bills, new customers were calling, and the red ink turned to black.

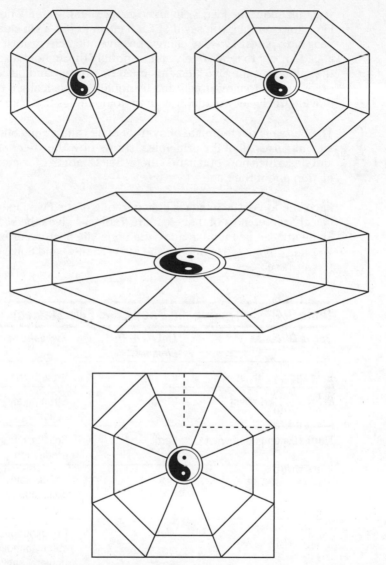

Figure 3-3: A squishy Bagua of your own.

Juggling Chi, Yin/Yang, the Bagua, and the Five Elements

Feng Shui's principles — chi, yin/yang, and the Five Elements — don't exist independently of one another. They're connected. When you talk about the Five Elements (Earth, Metal, Water, Wood, and Fire), for example, you say that each element has a yin side and a yang side. These types of energy, passive and active, must be balanced for chi to move freely and tranquilly throughout a space. In the same way, the Five Elements must be present and balanced in order for chi to move freely and tranquilly. So basically, if chi is moving freely and tranquilly, you're doing things the Feng Shui way!

The Bagua is the template or symbol of all things Feng Shui. It encompasses all of the principles, shows how they're connected, and describes how to balance them. See Chapter 1 for more information about the Bagua.

Each section of the Bagua is linked to one of the Five Elements, and has characteristics of that element. Table 3-4 gives the scoop. The Elements can be found in more than one Life Sector. For example, Wood is connected with both the East (Family) and Southeast (Wealth) sectors.

Table 3-4	Linking the Bagua and Five Elements	
Bagua Direction	**Linked to This Element**	**Symbolic of**
East and Southeast	Wood	Growth and new ideas
West and Northwest	Metal	Strength and purposeful action
Northeast and Southwest	Earth	Solidity, nurturing, and production
South	Fire	Enthusiasm and the completion and promotion of ideas
North	Water	Deep thought and a steady although not particularly active flow of energy

Too much yin or yang can make you feel uncomfortable. One of the Five Elements dominating the other elements can also make you uncomfortable. In still another way, a room can be out of balance even though it has all Five Elements present — if all Five Elements are represented in their yang aspect. Chapters 4, 5, and 6 discuss some approaches to out-of-balance workspaces. Part III has designs and ideas for specific kinds of workspaces, from cubicles to cars.

Balance all of the Feng Shui principles (the Five Elements, yin/yang, and chi) with your own intentions (goals you intend to accomplish) to create the most favorable, positive workspace.

Putting in the P.S. with Intentions

 Intention, the statement of your goal and purpose, is another important part of Feng Shui. It's not exactly magic that occurs when you put a dish of coins in your Wealth sector. What you're really doing is reminding yourself, every time you see that dish, that you're focused on creating wealth. For instance, say this as you place a lamp in the Fame sector: "By placing this lamp, a symbol of Fire, in the Fame sector of my office, I am enhancing my reputation in this company and in the outside world." It is this intention-setting process that does the major Feng Shui work.

Setting goals

When you use Feng Shui, focus on what you're trying to accomplish. Hanging bamboo flutes, a wind chime, and six crystals from your ceiling won't get you what you want unless you know what you want. That's where the power of intention comes in. You make the choice. You take control. You assume responsibility for your decisions. That's when Feng Shui is most effective.

 Your intentions can become affirmations that you use everyday to remind yourself to focus on your goals. Your affirmations should always be in the present tense. Tell yourself, "I am a successful businessperson," not "I will be a successful businessperson." Never underestimate the power of the present tense or the power of a focused intention. See Chapters 14 and 15 for more information on creating personal power and achieving your career goals.

Transcending your trashcan

Every act of Feng Shui has two aspects, the mundane and the transcendental. The *mundane* aspect is the practical part of Feng Shui. It's getting rid of the overflowing trashcan. The *transcendental* part is when you make the leap of faith and believe that by emptying the trashcan, you can bring a bit more order and efficiency into your life.

Mirror, Mirror

Mirrors are called "the aspirin of Feng Shui." They serve to deflect negative chi. On a subtle, energetic level mirrors are very powerful tools. Mirrors can be used to camouflage pillars and columns, which otherwise generate a lot of sha chi. They can be used outside and above front doors to keep negative chi from entering the structure. They can symbolically complete a space that is missing from the Bagua. Feng Shui mirrors are often eight-sided (called Bagua mirrors). These are the most potent, symbolically, but any mirror can be used to tell negative chi to "go back where it came from."

The use of mirrors can actually help make columns and square pillars visually "disappear." Department stores and restaurants often use this design technique for expanding the vista of clients when they enter a space plagued, for architectural and structural reasons, by pillars or columns.

Holly has visited the Airport Restaurant in Monterey, California on several occasions. Each time she is impressed with what the clever owner has done in a small space with a number of square pillars throughout — each one is completely mirrored with soft, pink smoke-tone mirrors. They reflect the great west view of the runway outside, double the food and the number of people within the rather small space. Diners relax with the abundant feeling of sunsets repeated within the room, and enjoy meals that are multiplied over and over. Such a delight!

Listening to your gut

Now you need to spend a few minutes getting in touch with your *intuition* (your insight or perception). This is the part of your mind that subtly makes you feel uncomfortable in a room painted entirely in red. Your intuition is an important ally in creating a Feng Shui workspace; it will tell you what works and what doesn't. Listen to what it's saying.

Figure out what makes your heart smile. Ask yourself some key questions and write the answers down, at a quiet time when you're away from your workspace:

- ✔ **How do I feel when I walk into my workspace:** happy, annoyed, or ready to work?

- ✔ **Is any element particularly annoying:** a squeaky chair, rollers that don't roll, that clock that chirps like a bird, or carpeting that trips me up?

- ✔ **Does anything create difficulties:** a stuck file drawer, a light in my eyes?

> ✔ **Are the objects arranged harmoniously or do they cause problems:** You constantly misplace files and you can never find a pen when you need one?

The answers to these questions give you a sense of the type of energy your workspace generates, and whether the way you've arranged objects helps or hinders you.

Now look at the layout you drew. Does it compare well with the favorable layout? Or does it look more like one of the unfavorable layouts? Mark any objects that appear to be positioned so that they interfere with the free flow of chi.

Now go beyond the mere arrangement of objects. Look at the whole picture of your workspace. Ask yourself questions like these:

> ✔ **Are the colors in your workspace harmonious and balanced?** Is the wall color neutral or at least balanced according to the Elements? Are the carpeting and window-coverings appealing? Does the design on your wallpaper make you seasick because so much is going on?
>
> ✔ **Does your workspace have lots of lighting, preferably natural, or does the lighting seem inadequate for your tasks?** A low-lit atmosphere is perfect for a nightclub, but not so perfect for accounting.
>
> ✔ **Is your workplace noisy or quiet?** Consider not just piped-in music and the loud conversations of your co-workers, but also the hum of the computer on your desk as it waits for you to use it.

Ask yourself how the space makes you feel: Lighter, less stressed? If it's a mess from top to bottom, list priorities to change it. If you feel mostly good about your space, but realize that you should have done something about that squeaky desk chair a long time ago, well, now you know what's high on your Feng Shui list!

Hold the Incense: Respecting Workspaces

You should always respect the fact that not everyone understands Feng Shui, and not everyone will agree that hanging wind chimes and spraying aromatics around the office will make it a more harmonious place to work.

Playing Yoda

Other people may resist Feng Shui because they don't understand what it is. They may tell you they "don't believe in" Feng Shui.

- ✔ Explain that you don't have to believe in anything to get the benefit of Feng Shui.
- ✔ Point out that Feng Shui is a design philosophy, not a religion.
- ✔ Describe how making the workspace more comfortable and welcoming will help make your work more enjoyable.
- ✔ Tell your boss or co-workers that simple steps, such as clearing the clutter, can make working less frustrating and annoying.

    You don't need to explain how this allows for the free flow of chi unless you think they're ready to hear that. Otherwise, just stick to the basics. Remind them that having a pleasant environment, one that appeals to all senses, contributes to better moods and less friction among co-workers.

Now you can say you gave at the office

Suppose your co-workers astonish you and say they want to Feng Shui the entire office, they love the smell of incense in the morning, and they can't get enough wind chimes to suit them. Now what?

Chimes or chairs first? Making priorities

Once you've got the go-ahead, determine what you need to do and in what order. It's best to start with the big-ticket items (so to speak). Clear the clutter, rearrange the furniture, and paint the walls if you can get away with it. Once the big jobs have been accomplished, move onto the smaller but still important tasks, like adding a crystal to your desktop or putting a mirror above your door: both are Feng Shui cures that can raise the good chi in your workspace.

Working a little OT

It's probably best to do your Feng Shui designing on your own time. If you're coordinating your efforts with co-workers, choose a Saturday afternoon (or other time when you're usually off and things are slow at the office) to get together and make some headway. Order in food and let each employee who wants to participate begin by clearing the clutter from her desk. This is just the beginning and it will give you a powerful jump-start to getting the entire workspace clutter free. You're on your way!

Tailoring your approach

So they've told you straight out that they want nothing to do with Feng Shui. Or they dismissed your explanations when you explained how they could benefit. If this is the case, be discreet about the Feng Shui you do.

- ✔ **Mum's the word.** If you're clearing the clutter to allow the free flow of chi, you don't have to tell your boss or co-workers that you're trying to ensure the free flow of chi. You can just tell them you're clearing the clutter to make the space more appealing. No one could argue with that!

- ✔ **Choose unobtrusive cures.** Instead of wind chimes that might make noise or aromatic scents that may drift over to the next desk, use crystals and mirrors to raise the chi. Use Bagua-shaped objects (such as an octagonal shaped planter) to enhance the chi.

- ✔ **Put a mirror in a drawer.** As long as you set your cure with intention, it will do its work even if you can't see it.

- ✔ **Wear it.** This is one of the easiest ways to feel comfortable and confident in your workspace. Turn to Chapter 15 for information about wearing your Feng Shui.

- ✔ **Use your imagination.** Accept that in some cases you will need to rein in your Feng Shui impulses and find creative ways to Feng Shui your workspace without offending co-workers.

Part II

Conceptualizing and Strategizing: Oddly at Peace with Peace

The 5th Wave   By Rich Tennant

"Oh him? I was feeling some disharmony in that corner of my cubicle and I couldn't come up with any wind chimes."

In this part . . .

In this part, we show you how to apply the principles of Feng Shui to any work environment. We give you strategies for using light, plants, and sound to raise the energy in your workspace and we give you the lowdown on using color and texture. We also dish up the dirt about the challenges of electronic equipment in the office.

You can discover tactics for curing Feng Shui challenges in any workspace, including what to do to prevent energy from getting blocked.

Chapter 4

Harmonizing with Light, Flowers, and Sound

• •

In This Chapter

▶ Making your workspace radiant

▶ Growing good chi with plants

▶ Creating a harmonious environment with music

• •

*F*eng Shui is about making a space feel good. Light, plants, flowers, and sound all play an important role in Feng Shui by creating the ideal environment. On the other hand, using these resources
inappropriately can create a tense, unpleasant atmosphere. (Think
of harsh lighting that glares off your computer screen, or music
blaring over the loudspeakers all day as you work at the record
store.) Using your Feng Shui tools with forethought helps create
the workspace that's right for you.

Lighting Up Your Life — Or at Least Your Workspace

Most people don't pay enough attention to the lighting in their
workspaces. If the ceiling light works when they flip the switch,
they call it good. But careful attention to lighting can brighten
your workspace and your life!

In Feng Shui, cures are objects that raise the chi. They can balance
out poor Feng Shui, but they can also encourage good chi even
when an environment already has good Feng Shui.

Light cures include any object that illuminates or lights up a
space — lamps, lighting fixtures, candles, a fireplace, and natural
sunlight all fall in this category. These represent the Fire element
and are symbolic of enthusiasm, passion, and high energy.

In this section, we talk about lights that illuminate, but don't forget that crystals and mirrors — even though they represent the Water element — can also add light, brilliance, and cheerfulness to a workspace!

Having a run-in with the sun

Sunlight is the best type of light for your mind, body, and spirit (just don't forget the sunblock for your skin!). Sunlight provides Vitamin D, which is essential for good health. Moonlight also helps your body! It's natural light; looking at the moon can help calm and relax you. So even if you work at night, you can still take advantage of natural light.

Windows and skylights are great, but no substitute for getting out there in the rays. To get the most from sunlight, you need to be out in it. Try to spend some time each workday outside.

Here are a few suggestions for getting out into the sun:

- ✔ Picnic on the grass outside your office building.
- ✔ Take a stretch break outside every few hours.
- ✔ Go for a quick walk around the block.

Feeling good about fluorescents

In Feng Shui, the basic rule of thumb is you can hardly have too much light in a workspace. (Obviously, if you work in a camera shop, this principle doesn't apply to the darkroom!) Although natural light is best, you probably need to supplement it with artificial lighting.

Although you can't have too much light, make sure the lighting in your workspace feels bright and pleasant — not harsh and glaring. To prevent light from glaring off your computer screen or the papers on your desk, filter it through blinds or other window coverings, plants, or anti-glare devices.

Spending too much time in artificial lighting without enough natural light can make you feel stagnant and depressed, reduce your energy, interfere with your sleep, and play havoc with your ability to work. People who spend most or all of their time in artificial light sometimes suffer from headaches, eyestrain, and increased stress levels. Make sure you get some natural light, too.

Sad?

Some people suffer from a disorder called *Seasonal Affective Disorder (SAD),* which causes them to feel depressed and sad in the wintertime. Getting more natural light can greatly help, but for those folks who simply can't get out in the day's rays, artificial lights can help too.

Quality lighting should be evenly distributed throughout the workspace. Having lighting only or mostly on one side of the room can make people feel uncomfortable.

It's best to combine three styles of artificial lights:

Overhead lighting

Overhead lighting brightens and illuminates an entire room, but can cast some areas of a space into shadow. For that reason, you also need to add area lighting and task lighting.

Area lighting

Area lighting illuminates a specific part of a room. Adding a floor lamp to a dim corner is an example. When placing area lighting, consider where the overhead lighting casts shadows and add area lighting to those places.

Task lighting

Task lighting focuses bright light on a small space as you do a specific task. For example, a desk lamp can help brighten up the space around your computer so that as you work at computer tasks, you don't suffer eyestrain. But task lighting does not illuminate a room in general. Place task lighting opposite the dominant hand so that shadows don't fall across your work.

Other types of lights you may want to use include:

- ✔ **Spotlights:** which can focus attention on a special piece of artwork.
- ✔ **Uplights:** which can increase brightness in areas where spotlighting can't be used. Uplights are less obvious and take less room than floor lamps.
- ✔ **Strip lighting:** which can be attached to the underside of an overhead cabinet and improve the lighting in a small area.

In addition to different styles of light, you may want to incorporate different kinds of light into your workspace. The following is a quick comparison of the kinds of light you can use:

- ✔ **Sunlight** is the best source of light. Windows or skylights are ideal light sources.

- ✔ **Incandescent lighting** has slightly lower levels of ultraviolet radiation than full-spectrum lights. It generally causes fewer problems (such as flickering and humming) than fluorescent lighting.

- ✔ **Fluorescent lighting,** although bright and cheap, emits higher electromagnetic fields than other lighting sources. The flickering and humming that some of these lights give off can cause stress and headaches.

- ✔ **Full spectrum lights** are more similar to sunlight than other types of artificial lights. Using these instead of incandescent or fluorescent lights can make you feel better and can cheer up your workspace.

Sending the Very Best to Yourself: Flowers and Plants

Think of how you feel in the spring when the gardens are blooming, the trees are leafing, and the world seems alive and vibrant. You can bring some of that color and life into your workspace by using flowers and plants. Even in the heart of winter, you can cheer your area up by keeping a fresh green plant on your desk or a vase of greenhouse blooms on your windowsill. If live plants aren't your thing, beautiful and vibrant silk plants work just fine!

Flowers and plants represent the Wood element and can

- ✔ **Camouflage corners and sharp edges.**
- ✔ **Prevent cutting chi from negatively affecting your space.**
- ✔ **Stimulate good energy.** You can use them in a dark corner or in an area that may otherwise accumulate blocked chi.
- ✔ **Help balance a dominant element.** For instance, you may have too much Earth energy in the form of the color brown in your space. A nice green plant can counteract that.

Dry, dead flower arrangements represent dead chi and are better off elsewhere. Dead or dying plants and flowers are worse than no plants or flowers at all. They drain good chi from the space and are uncomfortable and distressing to look at. Chapter 3 talks more about chi.

If you have fresh cut flowers in your space, be careful to take blooms out as they wilt and die. If you have potted plants and flowers, remove dead leaves and dead heads frequently. If a plant cannot be revived, give it back to the Earth with your thanks, and find another plant to take its place.

Choosing wisely

Plants and flowers send specific Feng Shui messages, so you have to be careful to select appropriate plants and flowers for your space. Additionally, some plants and flowers have cultural messages. Some folks think lilies are an attractive plant; but others see them as symbolic of death. Keep cultural meanings in mind as you select and care for plants in your workspace.

Here are some things to remember as you go in search of plants to liven up your space:

- **Sharp leaves** can create *sha chi* (cutting or negative energy).
- **Cacti** can make people feel uncomfortable and unwelcome.
- **Bright flowers and lush blossoms** are particularly effective as cures (energy enhancers) because they contain more vibrant chi!
- **Plastic and artificial plants** are not as powerful at raising chi as healthy live ones, but can be effective. If they must be used because of workplace regulations, allergies, or some other reason, make sure they're attractive, well dusted, and of high quality.

Choose the plant or flower for its specific qualities. Think of color, texture, smell, size and shape. Don't forget the meanings of plants. In China

- Bamboo symbolizes harmony and good fortune.
- Rubber plants symbolize good fortune.
- Chrysanthemums symbolize resolution.
- Gardenias symbolize strength.

✔ Jade plants symbolize good luck and wealth.

✔ Orchids symbolize endurance.

✔ Any evergreen, especially bonsai, symbolizes longevity.

✔ Money plants *(lunaria annua* or *crassula ovata)* symbolize abundance and wealth.

See Figure 4-1 for plants and flowers that have good Feng Shui energy.

Figure 4-1: The plants shown here are in good health, have rounded leaves, and project an appealing image. Don't forget to water them.

Placing properly

Plants and flowers create positive, energetic (vibrant) chi in your workspace. But you can't just stick them any old place and expect to get the best effect. (Remember, Feng Shui is a design philosophy and placement is an important part of design.) Because plants generate energy, placing them in the right Life Sectors gets greenery working on your side. See Chapter 1 for more information on Life Sectors.

The Bagua, Feng Shui's octagonal "map," is divided into nine Life Sectors, with each direction symbolizing a certain aspect of life, such as Career or Family. More on this in Chapter 3.

For example, if you have a post with sharp corners in your workspace, you need a tall, lush plant to camouflage it. The cutting chi emanating from the column may overwhelm a tiny jade plant.

If you're using the plant for a cure, make sure it's sufficient in size for that cure.

Don't hang plants directly over a doorway, a desk, or a chair. Energetically it makes you feel as though something is hanging over your head that can potentially do you harm, such as fall on you! Large vases with flowers or plants, weighty bric-a-brac, or any heavy design element hanging above you or on overhead shelving can make you feel energetically nervous.

A plant placed where an area of the Bagua is missing can raise the chi of the area and can energetically act to "complete" the sector that is missing. If the Wealth sector is missing, a plant placed near where the sector would be (if it existed) symbolically completes the sector.

Also, an odd number of plants are more aesthetically pleasing and more favorable than an even number of plants (but an even number of plants can be used). See Figure 4-2 for plant and flower placement.

Figure 4-2: Arrange plants near sharp edges to reduce cutting chi.

Soothing the Savage Beast with Sound

If you've ever been yelled at, then you know that the wrong kind of sound in the wrong place at the wrong time can be frustrating, annoying, and even harmful. But sound used correctly can be appealing, gratifying, and energizing.

In Feng Shui, gentle or tranquil sound can be a cure, by raising chi and making your space seem calmer and more pleasant.

Extremely loud noise, especially if it lasts for a long period of time, can damage your hearing. If you work around lots of noise, wear ear protection.

Ding dong, the chi is moving

Pleasant ringing sounds can be used at any time to raise the chi in an area. Ringing sounds can be used to

- **Moderate chi flow.** If chi moves too quickly through your space, sound cures can help slow it down.

- **Change chi's direction.** Soft background music playing from your cubicle can change the direction of the copy machine's drone — sending it away from you.

- **Dispel antagonism and negative energy in the workplace.** The gentle sound of a fountain can go a long way toward diminishing hostile feelings within a space and dispersing negative chi. Put a wind chime in the Family sector when a co-worker is sometimes loud on the phone. (The Family sector influences work relationships when you're at work.) Whereas a mirror deflects the energy completely, a wind chime moderates and reduces it. Your co-worker is performing a natural (although annoying!) action, so reducing the energy rather than negating it is appropriate.

Wind chimes are a common Feng Shui cure. Used outside, the wind moving through the chimes creates music. Inside, they ring as people move about. Or, you can deliberately make them ring as you walk by. Brass bells of various sizes can produce pleasing sounds and raise the chi.

Objects that ring have different pitches, tones, harmonies, and sound qualities. Listen carefully before choosing; only your ears can tell you whether the sound of the chime is pleasing or not.

Be respectful of your co-workers. They may find the wind chimes annoying, not energizing. Get permission first if you need it.

Playing some mood music

Music, like wind chimes and bells, can increase the chi in your workspace. Unlike wind chimes and bells, your co-workers are less likely to object to your playing music as long as it's soft and low. And if you're not allowed to play music out loud, many work places allow you to bring in your own portable music player and head-phones.

Depending on the decibel level and the cadence, music is thought to be yang in character, so when a space is too *yin* — too quiet and passive — music can energize it.

Match the music to your environment. A radio playing soft classi-cal music is suitable for most office work. (A tape of lullabies is too calming and you may find yourself needing a nap!) For creative or active pursuits, more energetic music can help generate good, active energy.

If you work where you don't have control over the music — the store where you work plays the Muzak version of Madonna's great-est hits all day, every day — ask if the volume can be lowered or if a different type of music can be substituted. If possible, add a Feng Shui sound cure, such as a wind chime, where you spend most of your working hours. See this chapter's "Easing Emptiness" for more information about this.

Easing emptiness

Noisy conversations, the clatter of the printer, the hum of your computer — all can raise stress levels and cause discomfort in your workspace. Blank walls, ceilings, and floors amplify sound, so adding materials to them creates a more pleasant environ-ment. Sometimes noise can be camouflaged with music or sound machines, but often this just creates another layer on top of the stressful noise.

What can you do? These tools can absorb disturbing background noises:

- ✔ **Colorful textiles hung on the wall.** See Chapter 5 for more information on color and texture.

- ✔ **Plants placed carefully.** See this chapter's "Sending the Very Best to Yourself," for more information.

- ✔ **Fountains flowing.** See this chapter's, "Honing in on rippling water" for more information.

Honing in on rippling water

The sound of moving water creates a pleasant, relaxed feeling (unless it's dripping from a leaky faucet). Water features such as desktop water fountains and aquariums are popular Feng Shui cures for a multitude of problems.

In Feng Shui, Water represents relationships, wealth, and general abundance; it is symbolically and literally necessary to life. The ideal locations for a water feature are the north (a Water area), the east, and the southeast (Wood element areas). Don't forget to set your intention as you place your water cures.

Your intention is what you want to accomplish by placing the cure. As you place your cure, remind yourself what it will do. For example, say something like, "By placing this fountain in my workspace, I signal my intention to reduce the amount of unpleasant noise in this area, which will make it easier for me to do my job." This mindfulness is just as important as the cure itself. See Chapter 1 for more information about intentions.

Is this thing on?!

Do co-workers flinch when you pick up the phone? Be aware of how much discomfort noise can cause and be respectful of others who share your space. Listen to yourself when you talk on the phone (a tape recorder can be a useful device if you can't really hear yourself). Do you speak in a calm, well-modulated voice? Or are you a loud and rapid talker? If the tape recorder doesn't help you moderate your voice, working with a speech coach just might do the trick. If that's beyond your means, have a trusted co-worker give you the heads-up with an agreed-upon signal when you start getting carried away.

Aquariums

Aquariums can be incorporated into many workspaces. Because they combine living energy and water, aquariums can be especially powerful. Aquariums bring good fortune and symbolize flowing chi that never gets stuck. An aquarium placed in the Wealth sector symbolizes abundance.

Don't rush out and get an aquarium unless you're sure you can follow these guidelines:

- ✔ **Healthy fish only.** Think robust — try to avoid the puny goldfish.

- ✔ **Ideally, plants are living.** Don't pick out the plastic plants you see at many pet stores unless you have no choice.

- ✔ **Aquariums need to be cleaned regularly.** Otherwise, they can create negative chi. And stink up your office too!

Want to get really fish picky? Nine is a favorable number in Feng Shui, so try to collect nine fish. Traditionally, one of the fish is black, to absorb the negative chi, and the other eight are gold. However, if you want to get along with a wide variety of people, it is more favorable to have fish of all different colors and sizes. If a fish dies, replace him right away.

Fountains and waterfalls

Flowing water symbolizes money flowing to you. Water features that perform work (as in a water wheel) are considered auspicious.

Desktop size water fountains and waterfalls

- ✔ Create energy
- ✔ Refresh your spirits
- ✔ Make visitors feel welcome
- ✔ Are calming

Don't place fountains and waterfalls in the Fame sector, as they may dampen the Fire element necessary to Fame. Be sure to keep the water fresh and clean with a drop or two of bleach every few weeks. And clean hard water calcium stains with a calcium remover product. If the water fountain gets dirty, not only does it create an unattractive sight but may create negative chi.

If for some reason you cannot use a water feature in your work-space, a painting of water also stimulates the chi! See Figure 4-3 for a look at a water feature just outside the window. Water features are also available in convenient desktop versions!

Figure 4-3: Gaze at your desktop to see this relaxing water feature!

Chapter 5

Brushing Up on Color and Texture

Color and texture are important tools for creating the workspace that's right for you. Both color and texture are visual; you can see a red wall and you can see a rough weave in a fabric like canvas. Texture also has the advantage of being tactile; you can feel it. Combining the two creates an experience of sight and touch that affects how you and others perceive your space. For example, a red velvet curtain creates a different feeling than a blue cotton curtain.

Color and texture appeal to the senses and have a mental and emotional effect on you and on visitors to your workspace. This chapter shows you how to use the tools of color and texture effectively. We show you how to select the right colors for you and your type of work.

Pulling Out Your Crayons

Colors affect your emotions, how much energy you have, and even how effective you are at what you do. Vivid colors like reds and oranges make you feel active. Less intense colors, like lavender, make you feel calmer. The term *hue* is frequently used to mean a gradation or shade of color.

Applying color to your workspace can help you achieve your goals, create energy and otherwise benefit you. For example, Earth colors — those that resemble colors found in nature, such as green and brown — are helpful because they symbolize grounding and stability and generate yin energy. Using Earth colors can help you feel grounded and connected at work. Feeling grounded is essential in high-pressure jobs, when you work long hours, or when stress is high for any reason.

You choose and use color to create balance in your surroundings. To make wise choices, you must understand how color is used in Feng Shui. In addition to the symbolic, culturally constructed meaning that you may already be familiar with, each color also has attributes that tie it into the Five Elements (see Table 5-1) and the nine Life Sectors on the Bagua (see Table 5-2). Chapter 1 describes the Bagua and the Life Sectors in more detail.

Balancing the colors in your workspace helps balance the chi. (More on chi in Chapter 3.) And that's a good thing. Just as too much of one element creates a lack of balance and can make you feel uncomfortable, too much of one color can also create a lack of balance. Strong, yang colors (such as bright red) create yang energy (or yang chi) and should be balanced with softer yin colors (such as pastel green) to create yin energy that balances the yang energy. Try to find ways to incorporate colors associated with all Five Elements into your workspace.

If you have too much of a particular element in your workspace, avoid the color associated with that element — you don't need it. One example is the Metal element. In most workspaces, Metal is found in abundance — your computer, your desk lamp, your picture frames all might be metal. White, the color associated with the Metal element, can and should be avoided.

Culture shock

Colors have cultural values attached to them. In Western cultures, white symbolizes purity, whereas in Eastern cultures, it symbolizes death. Black may symbolize death for some cultures, whereas for others, it's a sign of good fortune. Red signals danger in some cultures; in others, it's used for celebrations. Keep meaning in mind as you choose colors for your workspace. The following Web sites can help you learn more about the meaning of color in different cultures:

✔ www.princetonol.com/groups/iad/lessons/middle/color.htm

✔ http://library.thinkquest.org/50065/psych/meaning.html

Table 5-1 shows the relationship of color, element and attributes. Use this table to help you choose the right colors for your workspace.

Table 5-1	Color Elements and Attributes	
Color	*Element*	*Attributes*
Red	Fire	Happiness, power, luck, passion, fame, aggression, summer
Yellow	Earth	Stability, royalty, gaiety, patience, wisdom, autumn
Orange		Happiness, power, autumn
Green	Wood	Growth, inspiration, re-birth, eternity, harmony, spring
Blue	Water	Heaven, clarity of communication, spirituality, winter
Purple		High office, wealth, power, richness, spirituality
Gray	Metal	Ambivalence, frustration, ambiguity, hopelessness
White	Metal	Purity, precision, rigidity
Black	Water	Spirituality, intellectual depth, continuity, wisdom, winter
Brown	Earth	Stability, depth, endurance, autumn
Gold		Richness, power

Reinforcing your goals

Colors represent areas of the Bagua; you can use them to reinforce the goals you have set for yourself. (See Chapter 1 for more on the Bagua.)

For example, suppose you want to increase your wealth. Pay extra attention to the Wealth sector. Because greens and purples are associated with Wealth, you can paint the wall near the Wealth sector in your workspace violet, hang a piece of green art there, or tack a piece of purple paper there. (See, isn't this easy?)

To achieve your life goals, you need to understand which colors are associated with which area of the Bagua. Table 5-2 shows you.

Good luck

Holly was called to do a Feng Shui consultation for a couple specifically interested in improving their wealth and finances. Holly recommended they clear their wealth area of all clutter, place crystals in two windows, and set a purple pillar candle on a Bagua-shaped mirror on a table in that spot. She reminded them to set their intentions when they placed the cures. Several weeks later, they called to let Holly know a lawsuit had been decided in their favor, they unexpectedly inherited a large sum of money, and they won a substantial prize in a contest sponsored by a hobby club.

Table 5-2	Color on the Bagua
Color	*Life Sector*
Reds	Fame
Reds and pinks	Marriage
White and pastels	Children and creativity
Gray and black	Helpful people and travel
Black and dark colors	Career
Blues and greens	Knowledge, spirituality, family, and elders
Greens and purples	Wealth
Yellow and earth colors	Health and overall well-being

Whipping up some energy

Because color is closely connected to the Five Elements and to the flow of chi, you can use color to create the type of energy that you want to have in your workspace.

Most workspaces are high in yang energy — people are engaged in vibrant, active movement.

In general, the balance of yin and yang in a workspace should be slightly in favor of yang, because yang raises the energy and increases productivity. If you have to produce 1,500 widgets today, you don't want people on the production line to be taking naps. Creating a more yang workspace means using strong colors instead of less vibrant colors.

Color's yin and yang

Every color has a yin or a yang element to it. In balancing color in your workspace, remember that yin and yang need to be in balance, too.

✔ Pastel colors are yin.

✔ Stronger, more vivid colors are yang.

✔ Red is the most yang of all the colors.

✔ Orange is usually a yang color.

✔ Green, blue, and black are usually yin colors unless very bright.

✔ Yang colors create action.

✔ Yin colors relax people and make them feel more rested.

However, if your workspace is already pretty yang, you may want to limit your efforts to placing splashes of accent color to stimulate the flow of energy. And in areas where it's important to reduce the amount of energy generated, using yin colors is helpful. A doctor's waiting room is a good example of such an area. Lots of soft blues and purples make patients feel calmer while they wait.

In reception areas, shared offices, and communal areas it is generally good Feng Shui to use primarily neutral colors on the walls and in the large furnishings. This makes the energy in the area more yin, calmer. Enhancing neutral colors with small amounts of accent colors corresponding with the Five Elements creates a comfortable, attractive space that is in balance but that doesn't make anyone feel uncomfortable. For example, a reception room with beige walls could benefit from some artwork that incorporates colors associated with the Five Elements: green, blue and so on. Since the amount of accent color added is small in comparison to the amount of beige color on the walls, the energy in the room remains yin (passive and calm) but the added color creates visual interest so the room doesn't seem boring.

Hard edges and hard surfaces are yang; this can create a lot of tense energy. If your space already has a lot of hard edges and surfaces, use some yin color as a cure to tone it down.

Looking good in red (or blue or yellow)

The right colors for you and your workspace depend on many considerations, including what you're trying to accomplish in your work and your own personal preferences.

Knowing your style

We can offer suggestions on what colors are most favorable for you and why. But color choices are very personal. Everyone has favorite colors and colors they dislike. This is not wrong or irrational; it's human.

So when we suggest purple, and purple is a color you can't stand, don't use it! Remember that every color has many gradations and shades. Red, for example, includes colors ranging from light pink to deep burgundy. Any of these shades can work if you need to add the Fire element to your workspace but don't like crimson.

Collar color is irrelevant: What color is your work?

You may be a blue-collar worker, putting together automobiles, or a white-collar worker, figuring out how many automobiles your employer needs to sell. Either way, your work has a color.

Making do

Suppose you can't paint your walls or choose new carpet. You can add color in subtle ways:

- A painting
- A pencil holder
- A flowering plant
- An illustrated calendar
- A color photograph
- A painted frame

If nothing else, you can wear your Feng Shui! Choose wardrobe colors that incorporate the colors your workspace is missing. Chapter 15 talks more about personal Feng Shui.

If you're in a high-energy business, such as sales and marketing, you might choose lots of strong colors, even clashing colors, to generate strong, positive energy. Just be aware that such a workspace isn't very restful and can make some people anxious.

On the other hand, if you're in a calmer, lower-energy business (perhaps you're a therapist), you probably want your clients to be relaxed and feel comfortable, so you would choose more neutral colors, more yin colors, and colors that symbolize growth and knowledge, such as blues, greens, and earth colors.

Getting Next to Textures

Texture is an important tool in Feng Shui, and just like color, it can be used effectively to enhance the chi in your workspace. Every object has texture, whether smooth or nubby, slick or prickly. Texture, like color, has yin and yang aspects.

- ✔ Yang: Rough, prickly, sticky, bumpy, harsh, and solid
- ✔ Yin: Smooth, silky, velvety, moist, and slippery

As we mentioned in Chapter 4, plants that have spiked-leaves cause cutting chi. Think of how uncomfortable it feels to run your hand across a cactus. That's an unappealing texture! Now consider the textures that do appeal, that seem friendly and inviting — the feeling of leather or suede, for instance. See Figure 5-1 for appealing textures that can be used in a workspace to enhance chi.

Leather, lace, silk, brocade and other fabrics with distinct textures can be used in your workspace to create good chi.

Some textures are more associated with one of the elements than others. Table 5-3 shows the details.

Table 5-3	Texture Associations	
Texture	**Element Association**	**Idea**
Textiles, cloth, and granite and slate surfaces	Wood	Woven textures
Fur, leather, feathers, wool	Fire	Smooth leather or supple suede
Ceramic and earthenware	Earth	The smooth surface of a tile and objects the slightly rougher feel of a clay pot

(continued)

Table 5-3 *(continued)*

Texture	Element Association	Idea
Stainless steel, copper, iron and aluminum	Metal	A smooth marble texture or a slightly rougher stone surface
Smooth reflective surfaces	Water	Crystal, glass, or mirror

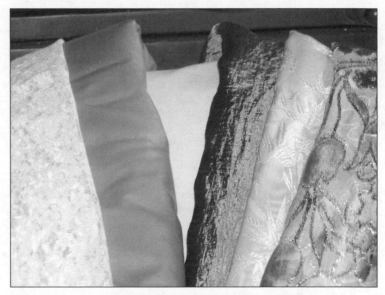

Figure 5-1: These textures can enhance chi in your workspace.

Texture also has yin and yang elements. Smooth, hard, shiny materials are yang. Energy moves off and through them quickly and directly. Use yang textures in areas where you don't expect (or want) people to linger — meeting rooms, bathrooms, cafeterias. Denser materials such as wood and upholstered furniture slow chi down and contain energy. They have a more yin aspect.

Applying Color and Texture to Floors, Walls, and Windows

As you analyze your workspace with Feng Shui eyes, start thinking in the language of the Elements. Ask yourself what you have to start with: neutral walls, brown linoleum floors, metal miniblinds, poor lighting, one small window, metal filing cabinets, metal desk, and a chair with minimal upholstery. Neutral, usually off-white walls are considered to be the Metal Element. Brown flooring is the Earth Element. Metal miniblinds are obviously Metal Element. Poor lighting is yin and small windows are yin. Eek! Give me more Earth, Water, Fire, and Wood!

Color + Texture / Flooring + Walls + Window Coverings = Balance

Shagadelic! Exploring flooring

Whenever you make a flooring choice, consider it in relation to what else is happening in the room. What other colors, textures and elements are you using? And what is the room used for? All will affect your flooring choice. Take a look at Table 5-4 for more information on flooring.

Table 5-4	Flooring and Its Elements
Flooring	*Element associated*
Ceramic tile	Earth
Carpet made of natural fibers (jute, cotton)	Wood
Carpet made of synthetic fibers (such as polyester)	No associated element
Wood	Wood
Laminate/Vinyl	No associated element
Marble	Earth

Practical considerations take precedence. In areas where water can splash around and make the floor slippery, consider placing rubber-backed mats on the floor, or using a rough-textured tile. If you have to stand for long periods, a hard tile surface is tough on your joints, and adding a carpet, or at least a rug, in the area where you stand most adds extra years to the life of your joints.

Rugging can keep you from bugging

Of course, you may not have much choice about the flooring in your workspace. Your new workspace comes equipped with smooth vinyl flooring, for instance. All is not lost. You can cover some of the flooring with a rug. You can even put a rug on top of carpet, if the carpet is unappealing.

Climbing the walls

Interior walls can dominate in a workspace. Glaring white-painted walls reflect a lot of light, make noise echo even more than usual, and otherwise make your space seem out of balance. Sometimes, the best thing to do is cover those walls.

When covering walls, consider what you're trying to achieve:

- ✔ **Control sound.** Add wallpaper and textiles (like wall hangings).

- ✔ **Slow chi.** Paint the walls using a texture brush for a rougher finish. You can choose wallpaper with natural texture.

- ✔ **Get rid of the glaring white look.** Painting the walls a neutral (but not white) color makes a huge impact.

- ✔ **Creatively balance the Five Elements.** If you need yang energy but don't want to paint all the walls red, or fear that this would create too much overwhelming yang energy, try painting three walls a neutral color and make a fourth wall an accent color. (Maybe this can be the wall behind your desk so that you don't have to see it all the time — otherwise you might feel too much yang energy!)

Can I get some privacy here? Window coverings

Although natural light is beneficial, sometimes windows let in too much light, causing glare. (Chapter 4 sheds some light on glare.) And sometimes a workspace has too much glass, making the room feel out of balance.

To solve these problems, use window coverings:

- ✔ Blinds
- ✔ Curtains
- ✔ Drapes

Always think natural. Cotton, ramie, and linen are better choices than polyester or plastic. All types of window coverings come in natural fabrics. Avoid synthetic materials whenever possible — not just because Feng Shui teaches that natural is better, but because health risks are associated with synthetic fabrics. See Chapter 7 for more information about health problems and synthetic materials.

When choosing window coverings, consider the room as a whole, and know what you are trying to achieve in your space:

- ✔ **Filter the light so it doesn't glare.** A light-colored cotton curtain provides translucent covering that removes glare.

- ✔ **Balancing high ceilings and echoing space.** Use a heavier fabric in a darker color and drape it to the floor.

- ✔ **Slow down chi.** Adding a drape in a dark color with a thick texture can slow fast-moving chi down.

Window coverings collect dust and get dirty. If you have them in your workspace, make certain they are cleaned routinely. Otherwise, they become a source of negative or tired chi.

Avoiding Too Much of a Good Thing: Balancing Color and Texture

Color and texture (along with other tools of Feng Shui) do not operate independently of each other. It's hard to have color without texture, and it's hard to have texture without color.

Always consider the whole. Bright colors and smooth textures may seem overwhelming in your workspace, and they may create too much yang energy. However, if your workspace already has too much yin energy, adding a bright color and a smooth texture will balance the yin energy out. Figure 5-2 provides a kind of framework for making Feng Shui decisions. Always remember to ask yourself how any element in your workspace makes you feel. And also try to figure out whether it's yin or yang.

Shedding some more light

Light plays a part in how you perceive both color and texture. A purple wall in a room with natural lighting might appear lavender in the morning, deep violet in the later afternoon. Texture is more apparent in lower lighting, whereas bright lighting can make texture seem to disappear.

Consider lighting as you design your workspace. When will you see the color and texture? Under what type of light? Make your color and texture choices under similar conditions. Bring samples of your material to your workspace before installing so that you can see what it will look like in its new home. See Chapter 4 for more information.

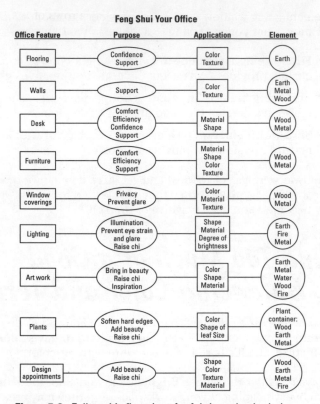

Figure 5-2: Follow this flowchart for fabric and color help.

Heavy Metal: Correcting the Overuse of an Element

In Chapter 1, we talked about the importance of the Five Elements, and how, ideally, they are all present and accounted for in your workspace. A good balance of all the elements creates favorable energy and is visually appealing.

However, it's very common for one element to dominate a workspace, causing subtle feelings of discomfort, and interfering with the balance of chi in a space.

Sometimes it can be hard to see what's wrong with a space. If you feel slightly uncomfortable, or if a workspace strikes a discordant note, and you don't see anything obvious like rows of bookshelves (cutting chi), spiked-leaved plants (subtly threatening), or the desk placed in front of a window (unsupported position), the problem might be too much of one element. Glance at Chapter 1 to refresh your memory about how the Five Elements work and to see how the elements interact.

Understanding why workspaces contain too much metal

Picture an office with a sleek metal desk, white walls, white uphol-stered guest chairs, an abstract painting of circles framed in a silver frame, and plants in brass containers. Seems sophisticated, doesn't it? But a workspace like this is a Feng Shui challenge. The overuse of the Metal element in this space may create an enormous amount of unbalanced chi.

Metal is a popular element in workspaces. Metal desks and filing cabinets are cheaper and more durable than their wooden counter-parts. Electronic equipment is generally made of metal or has metal elements and accents. Business sense dictates that you choose the cheaper, more durable item over the costlier, less permanent one. But excess Metal doesn't help workers feel energized and produc-tive. Metal chi is cold and dense; too much metal can contribute to feelings of rigidity and stubbornness. (Of course, Metal is associated with wealth, so don't dump all your Metal Element!)

And unfortunately, modern design emphasizes a high-tech look that incorporates sleek metal furnishings and silver and bronze accents. This attraction to metallic high tech is complicated by the fact that the color often used in these settings is white — the color associated with the element of Metal. So even those businesses prepared to shell out some serious bucks on office furniture and decoration frequently end up with too much Metal.

Metal is represented by the color white, and the season of fall. It is found in the Children and creativity sector. Shapes associated with it include the circle, sphere and dome.

Keeping metal in balance

If your workspace contains way too much metal, don't give up hope! You can balance the Metal element with a few simple cures — mostly by using other elements to balance the metal and make it more neutral.

The most powerful way to balance out Metal is to use Fire energy. Fire is related to summer, the color red, and the shape of a triangle. Adding red accents, such as a red throw pillow or a picture with strong red tones, to a space with too much metal helps create balance. The triangle shape in design accents reinforces the Fire element.

You can also use plants, which are Wood elements (Wood feeds Fire), to help balance the Metal. See Chapter 4 for advice on choosing the best plants and flowers for your needs (in this case, a flower with a vibrant red blossom is suitable, as it combines both Fire and Wood elements). Don't use brass planters or any type of pot that has metal accents. A clay or ceramic container produces the appropriate energy. Bring in some wooden furnishings or decorative touches.

 Avoid using the Earth element in a workspace with too much Metal element. According to the cycle of elements, Earth and Metal are closely connected (Earth feeds Metal). So, using too much Earth element can complicate the overuse of Metal! See Chapter 1 for more information on how the elements are related to each other. Figure 5-3 shows a fashionably high-tech room in need of balance. Plants will be added in strategic locations to counteract the metal, as will a natural fiber carpet. But the room already has black leather chairs that balance the metal and sliding glass doors, which reduce the amount of metal on the walls.

Figure 5-3: A metallic room in need of balance.

Chapter 6

Zoning In on Electronic Fixes

. . . .

In This Chapter

▶ Figuring out why electronic equipment gets on your nerves

▶ Washing that fax machine right out of your hair

. . . .

*Y*ou know how your shoulders get hunched closer and closer together as the day goes on? Until your muscles are so tense you can't even scratch your head over a puzzling problem without spraining your neck? Or how your headache gets worse and worse until you finally realize that it's the low hum coming from your computer that's driving you crazy? Or how when the air conditioner finally clicks off, your ears ring from the silence? Yes, indeed, you have electronic equipment to thank for all that. And you thought the most dangerous thing at work was the unfiltered water for your coffee!

But all these problems can be solved even if you can't fling that copy machine out the window. In this chapter, we show you how to tame that ever-present electronic equipment the Feng Shui way.

Getting the Buzz on Electronics

The annoying clicking sound the photocopier makes every time it completes a pass may be contributing to that nervous tick you recently developed. But what does that have to do with Feng Shui? After all, they didn't have microprocessors when Chinese emperors were first using the principles of Feng Shui!

Well, Feng Shui is the intentional design of your environment so that you feel welcome and comfortable when you're in it. If being at work gives you a tension headache three days out of five, it might have as much to do with the electronic equipment in your workspace as it does your office mate who bears a resemblance to Austin Powers! Anything that makes you sick or stressed, such as the electromagnetic radiation your computer gives off, is fair game for Feng Shui problem-solving.

Banging into the yang

Feeling comfortable in your workspace goes far beyond avoiding electromagnetic radiation and toning down loud noises. In fact, all of the electronic equipment and most of the office furniture in modern workspaces produces very yang energy. You knew there was a reason you wanted to smash that printer with a baseball bat!

Work areas tend to have a lot of yang energy anyway. If you don't have enough softening yin energy to balance the yang forces, you've got a Feng Shui challenge. When a workspace gets out of balance by having too much powerful yang energy, your health is at risk.

Yang energy overload can cause very real problems, including

- ✔ Extra stress
- ✔ Physical fatigue
- ✔ Difficulty finishing projects and other work
- ✔ Increased frustration and impatience
- ✔ Decreased attention spans

Electronic equipment and strongly cornered furniture with sharp angles continually pointing at you creates *sha chi* — negative, cutting energy that can drain your otherwise positive spirits and give you a feeling of being chastised. In addition, electronic equipment causes an excess of the Metal element in your workspace. See Chapter 4 for information on correcting that problem. Figure 6-1 shows a poorly designed workstation. First of all, facing a blank wall with your back to the door is not a power position. The person who sits at this desk may not be able to turn her desk around, but she could place a mirror so that she could see the door. And she should clear up the clutter on her desk and place the phone in the wealth sector to encourage business.

Figure 6-1: The disorganized piles on this desk make for bad Feng Shui.

A well-designed workspace appears when you

✔ **Put your computer on your desk, directly in front of you or slightly off to one side; but make sure it doesn't block your view of the door.** We know you hate it when your boss pops in unexpectedly, but isn't it better to see her coming? If you must place the computer where your back is to the door when you're using it, place a mirror at eye level so that you can still see the door.

✔ **Position the sharp angles and edges of equipment so that they don't point directly at you.** Shimmy furniture but watch your back.

✔ **Don't sit directly behind the back of a computer.** Most electromagnetic radiation comes from the back.

✔ **Have photocopiers and printers in a separate room.** Or at least place them a good distance away from you.

✔ **Avoid cradling the phone between your chin and shoulder.** This causes muscle tension and can even interfere with the flow of chi in your body! Instead, invest in a hands-free headset.

✔ **Make certain to get up and move around frequently — at least every hour or two.** (Instead of printing documents every now and then, save them up and print them all at the same time — while you're out of the office getting a breath of fresh air.)

✔ **Take notes by hand instead of using a Personal Digital Assistant (PDA).** You remember what a nice pad and pencil look and feel like, right? Chuck the electronic note makers.

✔ **Balance out all that yang with some yin.** Pick out yin carpets, curtains, wood, textured surfaces, and pieces of art. Don't forget that some activities are naturally yin, such as writing, producing, packaging, and administrative duties.

✔ **Wear natural fibers.** This reduces static electricity, which can be a big plus in a workspace overly endowed with equipment.

Polluting the air: What's that sound?

Most offices are filled with noise. People keyboarding, phones ringing, air conditioners or heaters clicking on and off, printers humming, and workers talking with each other.

All this sound creates an unpleasant work environment. How can you concentrate when you can't even hear yourself think? You may not be consciously aware of some of that low-level background noise, but you *do* hear it! On a subtle, energetic level noise can cause stress, anxiety, and frustration. On a less subtle level, all that noise can make you long for a vacation in one of those monasteries where no one is allowed to talk.

Health and safety concerns

Electromagnetism is magnetism developed by a current of electricity. If you pass a piece of metal through an electric current, it becomes magnetized. Radio waves, infrared, ultraviolet light, and X-rays are all examples of electromagnetic waves.

Electronic equipment produces electromagnetic fields, which are thought to create or contribute to health problems — electromagnetic radiation may suppress the immune system. It's best not to sit surrounded by wires and electric cables!

Electronic equipment also produces hazardous materials. The toner and ink cartridges used for copiers and printers can be toxic. Some of the chemical emissions are known to contain carcinogens. Use special care when handling the materials that go into these machines (and when handling the materials that come out of them, as well!).

And don't forget that improper posture at the computer can cause physical discomfort and injuries, poorly placed equipment can cause unnecessary physical strain, and doing the same task over and over can cause repetitive stress injury. And you thought construction work was more dangerous than accounting!

Anything that is energetically distracting, jarring, bothersome, or otherwise offensive to the senses is bad Feng Shui. This principle can be applied to almost anything in your surroundings.

If you can't talk your boss into assigning you the highly desirable corner office with the soundproofed door, you can still create a workspace that quiets the noise. Here are some tips on reducing noise:

✔ **Think practical.** Turn off the sound whenever you can. Shut down the printer if you're not using it, close your door, oil the squeaky desk chair, and use a Web fax service.

✔ **Create barriers.** An attractive screen not only camouflages an ugly radiator, it also quiets some of the rattles and gurgles.

✔ **Arrange your workspace so you're away from the source of noise.** Put your printer on the other side of the room — and hide that cable! Keep your desk a few feet away from windows and doors.

✔ **If you're sharing a space with another person, place your desks so they are not side-by-side.** Allow plenty of room between the two. That way, your co-worker's noise doesn't combine with yours and distract both of you.

✔ **Make certain that pathways allow free movement.** Pathways should be kept clear of clutter so people can easily move around. Don't let arrangements force them to congregate in front of your desk on their way out to lunch.

✔ **Remember textiles.** A rug or carpet on the floor helps deaden sound. A wall hanging keeps sounds from echoing off the walls. Window coverings can keep outside noises from adding to inside noises. See Chapter 5 for more information about color and texture.

✔ **Lower the ring volume on your phone.** If you can't figure how, read its manual or ask your neighbor. Or put your hand over the ringer every time it goes off.

✔ **Bring in some plants.** Green plants absorb noise and keep the sound down. They also relax you and calm you with their beauty. Plants that clean the air include:

- Rubber plants

- Peace lilies

- Philodendrons

- Boston ferns

✔ **Bring a small, good-quality CD player or radio.** Have soft, classical music playing in the background. The trick is to keep the music low so that people don't feel they have to compete with it. Consider using headphones.

✔ **Purchase a white noise or sound machine.** These machines may emit a low background noise or produce the sound of rushing water to help relax you.

✔ **Add a water feature.** The sound of real water can cover up other sounds. The pleasure of seeing the water also adds a relaxing dimension to the experience.

✔ **Invest in noise-reducing headphones.** These eliminate most background, ambient sounds, but you can still hear someone speaking directly to you.

✔ **Use earplugs.** Invest in some earplugs if you work in areas with loud noise to protect yourself from permanent hearing loss.

Toning down

Every company has one, the friendly co-worker whose laugh shakes pictures off the walls, the salesman who booms, "Good morning!" to everyone he meets, the employee whose phone conversation is so loud you know every detail of her last operation. None of these people is trying to ruin your day. They're just loud.

So what can you do besides shout, "Keep it down in there!"?

✔ **Go the polite route:** If you feel comfortable talking with the person yourself, you can say, "Joe, sometimes I think you don't realize how hearty your voice is! When you're on the phone, it can be hard for me to concentrate. Do you think you could take it down a notch or two?"

✔ **Try an appeal to your boss or his boss:** Suggest that a little volume control might be a good thing. Instead of saying, "Joe drives me crazy when he gets barking on the phone!" you might phrase it in more general terms, such as, "I'm thinking of the appearance we portray to clients. Sometimes things get pretty loud in here when some people get on the phone. Can we encourage a more professional image?"

✔ **Be subtle:** Create a needlepoint sign for your cubicle wall that says, "Silence is Golden."

✔ **Model good noise control yourself:** If your voice has a tendency to get louder the more excited you get, and you get excited a lot, you can hardly complain when a co-worker does the same thing. Practice modulating your voice (speak into a tape recorder to get some objective feedback). (Recording Joe on the phone and then playing it back to him to prove your point is not good Feng Shui.)

Tripping you up: Cords

The last time one of us upgraded her computer equipment, she counted seven electrical cords hooked up to two power surge protectors, four different cables attaching various pieces of equipment to various other pieces of equipment, and three phone lines — and this didn't even include the phone's handset cord, the electric calculator, or the lamp.

See Figure 6-2 to get a glimpse of what too many cords and cables looks like, and see if you can relate. Who hasn't spent fifteen minutes tracing a power cord back to its source only to find it's the wrong one?

Figure 6-2: Visual snakes consist of cords and cables. This tangle of cords and cables is visually unappealing and may seem subtly threatening.

All those cords and cables are like *visual snakes* — unattractive, unappealing, and even subtly threatening. Energetically cords and cables signal clutter and tangle: not the free and easy movement of chi. And cords and cables can literally trip you up as they spill across the floor trailing their way to the nearest electrical outlet. They're definitely not friendly and inviting to people popping into your workspace.

But because it's impossible to give the computer away to a worthy cause and go back to the manual typewriter, we've included some advice for dealing with those snake-like cords.

Kicking strain in the rump with ergonomics

Ergonomics — the modern science of designing and arranging objects so people can interact with them efficiently and safely — is a useful new partner to classical Feng Shui. Just as Feng Shui shows how to place objects most favorably, ergonomics shows how to place them most safely. In other words, your computer monitor should be set at eye level, your chair should support your back, and your phone should be within easy reach. Equipment, from chairs to keyboards, is being designed with ergonomics in mind.

Doing the same tasks over and over (such as typing for hours on end) can cause *repetitive stress injury (RSI).* That's why any discussion of creating a comfortable workspace requires you to make some adjustments in *how* you work. It doesn't matter how well placed your computer is if you don't move from your chair now and then.

Given that electronic equipment can create physical problems in workers, you may be able to convince the powers-that-be to give Feng Shui a try in your company. Remind them that the bottom line is fewer sick days and a healthier, happier workforce. What manager wants more?

For more information about ergonomics, see www.osha.gov/SLTC/ergonomics or www.ergoweb.com.

- ✔ **Purchase cord tubes.** This device fits over bundles of cords, camouflaging them.

- ✔ **Buy a desk designed with holes cut for cables to fit through.** These desks have predrilled spaces to thread cables and cords through so that they don't snake all over the top of your desk.

- ✔ **Move a piece of equipment to another area.** The further away from you, the better!

- ✔ **Decide whether you need all of that equipment in front of you all the time.** Can you use one multifunction machine instead of a printer, scanner, fax machine, and copier? Can you share a printer with your office mate rather than each of you contributing a cable to the clutter?

Designating Equipment-Free Zones

One of the healthiest things you can do for your workspace is create some areas where electronic equipment is strictly forbidden.

✔ Take the microwave out of the lounge and turn the lounge into a neutral zone.

✔ Rearrange certain offices or gathering areas so that no equipment is allowed.

✔ Create small zones in your own workspace where equipment is not allowed.

✔ Add a "No computers allowed!" sign to the break room door.

Designating equipment free zones is one idea that your employer may appreciate. Explain that having a break room or area set aside where people can get away from the electronic equipment reduces stress and help increase productivity. Offer to oversee the removal of equipment from the break room personally if you think it will help!

If your boss or manager turns a deaf ear to your Feng Shui suggestions, point out the problems that created the out of balance chi and tell her how these problems affect the bottom line. An overly yang office creates a lot of stressed-out workers who can't get much done and who spend their time bickering with each other. Not something that any boss wants!

Part III

Energizing and Feng Shui-ing Your Work Area

The 5th Wave   By Rich Tennant

ROBERTA ADJUSTS THE FURNITURE IN HER OFFICE TO ACCOMMODATE A SALESPERSON

"Mike, so nice to see you again. Please, have a seat."

In this part . . .

Not everyone has a corner office (we both wish we did!). So we created this part to show you how to apply Feng Shui principles to specific types of workspaces. Whether you work in a cubicle, an open concept office, or a warehouse, we have strategies and ideas to help you bring out the best in your environment.

In this part, you can also find plenty of advice on correcting problem layouts and enhancing your career success. You find out how to plan the perfect Feng Shui office and how to handle the less-than-perfect workspace you probably have. You also find tips for creating awesome home offices, and for handling break rooms, conference rooms, and similar spaces.

Chapter 7

Building a Business the Feng Shui Way

*I*f you're lucky enough to be in charge of starting up a business — whether as an office manager, company president, bootstrap entrepreneur, or small business owner — you can create a Feng Shui workspace from the very beginning stages. This improves your chances of success, no matter what business you're in.

Making your work environment Feng Shui–friendly helps workers and clients feel comfortable and welcome, improves morale, communicates a positive business image, and increases your bottom line!

This chapter shows you how to Feng Shui all aspects of your business — from planning the layout of your building to choosing the stationery and logo. So no matter what stage you've reached in the process of growing your business, you can reap the benefits of following this classical art of placement.

Starting from Scratch

If you're able to start from the very beginning — choosing the location and design of the building (and maybe even deciding on the name of the company), you can tip the balance in favor of business success by applying the principles of Feng Shui to your selection process.

Creating a favorable Feng Shui environment begins with choosing the locale for your building, taking into consideration other nearby buildings and the natural environment. Then you move to the interior and choose how to layout the rooms in your space, what color to paint the walls, and where to stick Joe from Accounting.

Take the lead by creating a more natural office environment where people are happy to arrive for work every morning.

Picking the best locale

As any real estate agent can tell you, when planning a business, the most important consideration is location, location, location. While some people may believe that the perfect site is important only for retail shops needing high visibility, location is of vital importance in all business endeavors, whether dependant on walk-in clients or not. Everyone knows that a shop that specializes in selling clown accessories does better located next to the neighborhood clown college. But have you stopped to think that the local clown psychiatrist might do well to set up shop there as well?

Consider the things presented in Table 7-1 when choosing your building or figuring out where you want to build it.

Table 7-1	Selecting Building Locations	
Element	*Considerations*	*What you should do*
Weather	From which direction does most severe weather come?	Select a site that protects the entrance from bad weather.
Land formations	Where are the rivers, mountains, or plains in comparison to your locale?	If possible, choose a site that has rear and side protection and a view of a water feature such as a river or lake in the front.
Land shape	Is the parcel square or irregular?	Regular shapes are preferred.
View	What do you see from your locale? Is it pleasant?	Location is everything . . . don't settle for a location where your view doesn't make you feel good.

Element	Considerations	What you should do
Nearby buildings	What do they look like? How are they situated?	Try not to be "overshadowed" by significantly taller buildings around you. Look carefully for *sha* chi — negative arrows from any neighboring structure. If possible stay away from high power lines and large transformers.

See Figure 7-1 for an example of an auspicious building site.

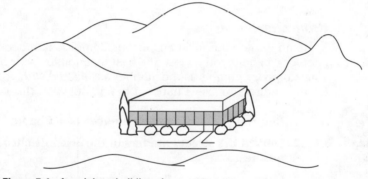

Figure 7-1: Auspicious building site.

A building site that resembles the back, seat, and arms of a comfortable chair is considered auspicious and is termed the *classic armchair position*. The building is positioned in the protected area where the seat meets the back. See if you can spot similar auspicious sites in your area.

The armchair location is ideal for homes and certain types of businesses. But for most work environments, a more favorable location is more exposed and accessible to the outside world than the armchair position. This position could be further up the mountain where the building would be more obvious to passersby, or toward the edge of the "seat," where the building could be seen from the road. To balance the yin and the yang energy, avoid areas that are too protected or too exposed. Some work environments that don't rely on outside traffic can be kept in the armchair position — for example, a warehouse would be protected in that area. Or, a home office could be situated in a house that rested in the safe armchair position.

85% chance for Feng Shui tomorrow

In China the worst weather and the most powerful storms come from the north. Ancient practitioners of Feng Shui laid out building sites on a north-south axis and positioned the rear of the building to the north in such a way as to create both protection and stability. The most favorable site was one with a hill behind the structure providing strength, support, and protection from the elements. Gentle land formations on both sides with protective areas of trees and other plants also provided nurturing support for the structure. In front, a much smaller, gentle hill — not high enough to block chi from entering the site — was favorable. A pleasant view and a water element, such as a pond or stream in the front, were also considered auspicious.

Using street numbers

Remember that your most auspicious Compass number or Gua number can help you choose the best location for your business. Your Compass number is the number associated with your most favorable direction. See Chapter 1 to find out what this is.

1. **Determine your Compass number (see Chapter 1).**

2. **Look at the street numbers of the possible sites for your business.**

3. **Choose one that reflects your most favorable number.**

   In other words, if your Compass Gua number is 9, open up shop at 9 Apple Avenue.

4. **If the street numbers are long, add them together to reach a number under ten.**

5. **Keep adding the numbers together until you reach a number between 1 and 9.**

   For instance: 1829 Oak Street

   $$1 + 8 + 2 + 9 = 20$$

   20 becomes $2 + 0 = 2$.

   If your Compass number is 3, a better bet is 1830 Oak Street ($1 + 8 + 3 + 0 = 12 = 1 + 2 = 3$).

6. **Compare the number with your Compass number.**

   If it matches your Compass number, then it's an auspicious site. If not, you may want to look further to find a site that matches your Compass number.

You can also strive for a location where your front door is oriented toward your most auspicious direction. (Refer to Chapter 1 to calculate your most favorable direction.)

However, please remember that even if your Bagua Number is 9 and an address of 666 ads up to 9, you probably don't want to locate your church at 666 Evil Street.

Creating a site plan

Once you've confirmed that the site number matches your Compass number (or if you decide you can live with the site's number clashing with yours), you can further evaluate whether a potential location is favorable by drawing a site plan. This sketch needs to include all relevant features, but it doesn't have to be complicated or even professionally drawn. All you need is yourself, your crayons, and a sketchpad.

1. **Indicate where your building is located.**

2. **Show terrain features.**

    Include other buildings, streets, hills, and structures such as water towers, radio and cell phone towers, highways, bridges and overpasses that might affect the flow of chi around your building.

    Include significant power lines, transformers, or any large electrical facility nearby.

3. **Look at the drawing with Feng Shui eyes.**

    Is it subject to any negative chi?

    Will nearby trees or buildings block chi from entering your space?

Will any other problems make the location less than ideal? See Figure 7-2 for an example of creating a site plan. It shows nearby buildings and natural formations that should be taken into consideration when choosing a site.

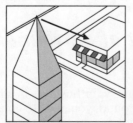

Figure 7-2: Creating a site plan.

Staying away from inappropriate locales

Feng Shui teaches that a building at the very top of a hill is energetically unsupported and open to buffeting on all sides by Mother Nature. Locating a structure on top of the highest peak in the area with a perfect view may seem ideal, but think again. Even though such a site seems to say, "Look at me!" thereby attracting the attention of potential customers, it's actually a very vulnerable location and one you may want to avoid.

Locations that present particular Feng Shui challenges:

- ✔ **Sites facing a busy highway:** All the chi flows quickly away. Busy streets are like rushing rivers of chi. The energy moves so fast that clients have to fight the constant rush of traffic and may have a hard time finding you. They may end up waving "bye-bye" as they fly past, unable to slow for the turnoff in time.

- ✔ **Structures located at or near a dead end:** Can act like a trap and not allow the beneficial chi to keep moving and circulating. Also, think symbolically: "dead" end?

- ✔ **Buildings directly facing straight roads:** At the top of a T-junction or at the top of a cul-de-sac. Oncoming traffic and headlights aimed at your building constantly send negative arrows of *sha chi* (cutting chi) straight toward you. And occasionally a car may miss the curve and careen directly into your front door. Not the kind of visitor you want to encourage.

- ✔ **Areas with strong water such as a river at the rear or water that rushes away from the building in a straight line:** This symbolizes the wealth flowing away from you. However, water in the front can be very favorable.

If your business does not rely on clients and customers visiting the building, you can choose a less accessible location, but you still want to avoid situations that generate negative or cutting chi.

Judging the impact of surrounding structures

Because you're probably not locating your business in a rural location without neighbors for miles around, you need to consider the impact of human-made surroundings as you select the most appropriate site for your business.

Think of how your building fits into your general area:

✔ **How big is your building compared to those around it?** For example, if towering buildings surround your small building, you may feel overshadowed and overpowered.

✔ **Do power lines, powerful radio towers, and transformers surround the building?** These structures send out a great deal of strong, negative chi. Also, they produce electromagnetic emissions, which may be hazardous to your health (see Chapter 6 for more information on health hazards of electromagnetic emissions).

✔ **Are graveyards and hospitals nearby?** The energy they generate is too yin to benefit most businesses, and may send a negative message of death and sickness to workers and clients. Churches, temples, and monasteries also send out large quantities of yin energy, so unless you are in the mortuary business or sell temple bells, it's best to avoid locating too close to them. (If the building doesn't face your front door, the problem is less serious.)

✔ **Does a building opposite yours have sharp angles or a very pointed roofline aimed directly at you?** This sends cutting, sha chi toward your front door, which is not favorable. It is also not fortunate to be located opposite a building that appears energetically threatening for any reason, such as the county lock-up or a bankruptcy counselor!

✔ **Where are the taller buildings located in comparison to your building?** Behind your site can be favorable (it's like having a hill or mountain behind your structure, offering support and protection). But tall buildings in front can block benevolent chi and feel overpowering and threatening as they cast shadows across your front door.

✔ **What's the energy of the overall neighborhood location?** Are other buildings run down, seedy looking, or defaced? Is trash left on the street and weeds not pulled? Do empty lots symbolize the lack of energy in the area? Was the previous business located in this spot similar to yours? And was it successful or did it prove to be doomed in this location? If Bob Joe's Used Cars for Less couldn't thrive, then Jimmy John's Junkers may not do so well either. Negative predecessor energy can create problems in your business and your establishment may suffer from guilt by association. See Chapter 14 for more information about this.

See Figure 7-3 for typical examples of building sites to avoid. The drawing marked A shows a building with its main doors blocked by a new expressway ramp. Drawing B shows a building "hit" by the sharp pointed roof design of the opposite building. Drawing C shows a smaller building that is sure to be adversely affected by the larger buildings near it. Drawing D shows a building that faces a T-junction. This kind of straight road pointing at the site is bad Feng Shui, because it creates cutting chi.

Awareness and being in touch with your feelings are both fundamental to this site selection process. Allow yourself to really *feel* how a specific location affects you. Understand and accept that your intuition may be trying to tell you something about this site. Continue looking. If you can't find another location that is energetically more empowering for you, determine if you can do anything to cure the dis-ease affecting you (see the "Curing Unfavorables" section later in this chapter for more information). If you feel genuinely enthusiastic and excited about a certain location, that's an important consideration, even if the front door faces an inauspicious direction.

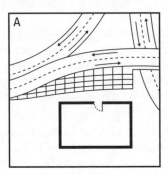
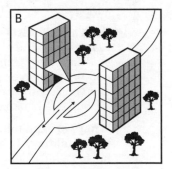
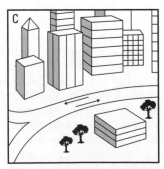
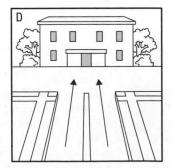

Figure 7-3: Poor building sites.

A less than ideal location doesn't have to be the end of your business. You can raise the chi (and raise awareness of your business) by using flags, banners, balloons, cheerleaders, wild dogs, or any attention-getting device that is appropriate to your company or trade.

Curing Unfavorables

All is not lost if you don't have any choice over your business location or something has happened to make your location unfavorable. You can add *cures* to help generate good chi at your location and to enhance your chances of success.

- ✔ **Washing bad chi right outta your hair.** If the front walk is in disrepair, the wastebasket by the front door is overflowing with trash, and piles of windblown leaves are stacked against the walls, it doesn't matter how auspicious your location — clients, workers, and visitors are unfavorably impressed by their first introduction to your business, and they wonder what else about your work is not being attended to! Not only is this kind of mess and clutter unfavorable from a Feng Shui standpoint (which, as a design philosophy, is about creating attractive spaces), it may also signal the accumulation of dead chi, or may cause chi to stagnate.

- ✔ **Completing the Bagua.** Irregularly shaped lots can be symbolically cured by adding lights to illuminate the missing areas. (See Chapter 1 for more information on the Bagua.) Trees or other landscaping can hide or augment these missing areas. See the section, "Planning a Specific Business," for more information on applying the Bagua to your building.

- ✔ **Calming cutting or negative chi.** See Table 7-2 for some chi problems and solutions.

Table 7-2	Chi Troubles and Cures	
The obstacle	*The resulting problem*	*The cure*
A single tree is in front of and too close to your main entrance.	Can send blocking, negative chi toward your business.	Add several other trees to the one in front. A single tree can thwart benevolent chi; a group of trees is energetically gentler.

(continued)

Table 7-2 *(continued)*

The obstacle	The resulting problem	The cure
A building opposite yours has sharp corners.	Creates cutting chi.	A Bagua mirror placed outside above your front door can deflect cutting chi.
A transformer or radio tower has been erected across the street from your site.	Creates negative chi and possibly unhealthy electromagnetic impulses.	Plants and other growing things can help protect your building.
Busy streets in front of your building or a street moves traffic directly toward your building.	Chi moves turbulently or too swiftly.	A man-made pond or reservoir creates good energy as long as it doesn't stagnate. A fountain placed near the front entrance can counteract negative chi.
Tall building in front of yours.	Blocks benevolent chi and feels overpowering and threatening.	Place a low structure in front to help protect your building; the structure should allow chi to flow gently toward your site.
For security you must have a wall or gate in front of your building.	Prevents chi flow.	Use gates or wrought iron fencing with openings.

✔ **Preventing chemical sensitivity.** Just as people get sick, some buildings get sick, too, and that's plain dangerous for the people who have to work in them.

- Use natural building and decorating materials whenever possible. Instead of vinyl, use ceramic tiles or natural fiber carpeting. Use linen drapes instead of polyester.

- Replace windows that don't open with windows that do.

- If your building does have windows that open, open them up now and then!

Even natural materials can cause blocked chi if they're not kept clean and in good repair. Regular maintenance and strict adherence to cleanliness are important parts of keeping your building and its occupants healthy and well.

Sick building syndrome: It's out there!

Sick Building Syndrome is a sad reality and can affect people with a number of physical ailments, among them multiple chemical sensitivity (MCS). MCS is a collection of symptoms similar to an allergic response that some people develop because they work in buildings built or decorated with toxic substances and without adequate ventilation. People suffering from this syndrome can develop (among other problems) headaches, intestinal problems, and rashes and they may exhibit signs of mental confusion.

In Feng Shui it is thought that the inadequate flow of chi contributes to this problem. The best treatment is prevention — making sure that buildings have windows that open and that natural materials are used whenever possible. Feng Shui cures may help by symbolically opening up blocked chi. Keep pathways clear, move furniture so that forward progress is not blocked, and use crystals, lights, and mirrors to encourage the free flow of chi.

Sick Building Syndrome is a real problem — and it can be very serious for workers. (See the sidebar "Sick building syndrome: It's out there!" for more information about this.) To get help in identifying and treating Sick Building Syndrome, check out the Environmental Protection Agency at www.epa.gov or the Indoor Air Quality Institute at www.sick-building-syndrome.net.

Designing Your Workspace the Feng Shui Way

After choosing a location, you must then construct the building. Well, you don't have to construct it yourself, but you get the idea. The building's overall shape and the placement of certain departments within the building are important Feng Shui considerations.

Building the building

Feng Shui design principles state that buildings should be regularly shaped. So pick a building shaped like a square or a rectangle, not like an amoeba. Incorporate natural elements as much as possible. For example, a brick, stone, or even stucco facing on the exterior of the building is good use of one of the Five Elements. The total number of floors doesn't matter, although nine is an auspicious number. Avoid placing front doors and back doors directly in line with one another, and place staircases away from the entrance so the chi doesn't go up the stairs instead of circulating on the ground floor area. Ensure that the entrance door doesn't open onto a wall, which is very unwelcoming.

 If your building was constructed before you converted to Feng Shui, and is missing a part of the Bagua, you can cure the area. Place one or more of the following where the missing corner would have been:

- ✔ **A bright light on a tall lightpole outside.**

- ✔ **A flagpole with a flag or banner.** It can have the same color as the color associated with the missing Bagua area. See Figure 7-4 for an example of how to do this. (Green is always effective because it symbolizes healing, new growth, and inspiration. The flag or banner could show the company's logo superimposed on a green background.)

- ✔ **A rock or statue.** These strong design elements act as an energetically grounding force but need to be substantial to make up for the missing area.

- ✔ **Plants, trees, and bushes.** Plant flowers in the color associated with the missing Bagua area.

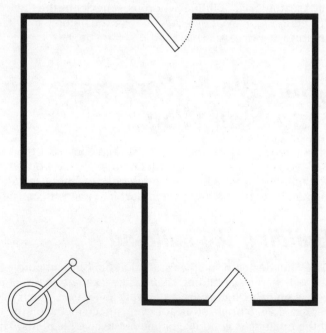

Figure 7-4: This flag raises the chi in the building's missing corner, symbolically completing it.

You can always combine more than one cure. Remember to set your intention as you place your cure. See Chapter 1 for more on intentions.

Putting accounting where it counts

Use the Feng Shui Bagua to determine the most auspicious locations for various departments and to ensure that a vital area (such as the Wealth Sector) is not missing entirely.

If your workspace is irregularly shaped, it may have at least one wall with an area that protrudes. This protruding area might be a little alcove or a weird little corner where the elevator shaft has cut into your space. If the protrusion — the part extending — is less than half the size of the total wall in question, it's considered an extension. Extra chi accumulates there. This is a good thing! Look at the illustration on the right in Figure 7-5 for a visual. However, if the protrusion is more than half of the wall space, it's not a protrusion after all, but in fact part of the space is incomplete. If you were to place the Bagua over the layout of your space, some part of the Bagua would be missing. Not auspicious. Check out the illustration on the left in Figure 7-5 to see what a missing piece looks like.

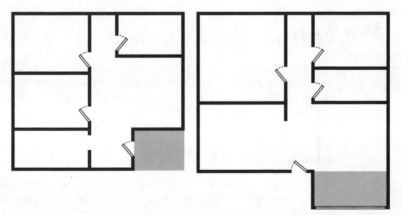

Figure 7-5: The illustration on the left shows a missing area in the floor plan; the illustration on the right shows a projection.

Symbolically complete the missing space with

- ✔ Mirrors
- ✔ Wind chimes or crystals
- ✔ Green plants

See Figure 7-6 for an example of a favorable floor plan for a business.

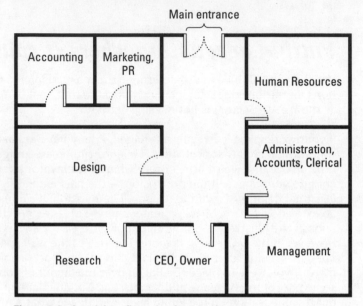

Figure 7-6: Auspicious floor plan for a business.

Projecting Your Image

The sign outside your business (or attached to the side of the building) conveys more than just the company name. It also communicates to potential clients qualities about your company image. It's best if these qualities are positive!

Looking into logos

Your company logo is almost as important as your company name. It communicates your image and what you want clients and customers to think about you.

Create a well-balanced logo that uses the principles of Feng Shui to bring customers hotfooting to your door. Check out this list for some pointers:

> ✔ Make the image on a logo clear and easily identifiable (even if it's an abstract design). You don't want customers to confuse your logo with someone else's. If the business next to

yours sports a logo of fighting weasels, avoid using even one sleeping weasel on your logo. Perhaps a sleeping koala would be more appropriate.

✔ Avoid unattractive, unpleasant, or threatening images. A logo of a sharp knife is an example of an unpleasant image that may actually deter people from entering your business. Even if you sell knives for a living, a picture of a smiling chef chopping celery would be more likely to draw people in.

✔ Shapes and symbols matter. An arrow pointing up symbolizes growth, and is acceptable, but arrows pointing in other directions can send cutting chi out into the world. Square shapes represent solidity; circles symbolize wholeness and unity; these are favorable designs for company logos.

✔ Color matters, too. Whenever possible choose colors and shapes to incorporate the Five Elements and a symbolic message of professionalism you want people to associate with your business.

Reproducing a color logo in black and white reduces its effectiveness because the vibrant chi of color is no longer there. Also, incorporate the Five Elements into your Web site whenever possible. Most of all, keep it clutter-free! If a potential client clicks on your site and is confronted by an array of pictures, banners, and dancing bananas he will leave.

Signs, signs everywhere

Signs are often the first impression a visitor has of your business. A person driving by may catch a glimpse of your sign and mentally file it away for future reference.

Designing

A sign should represent the principles of Feng Shui just as a workspace does. Including the Five Elements is just as important in a sign as it is in your boardroom. Pay attention to the list below as you design (or have someone design) signs for your business.

Shapes are very significant in Feng Shui and relate directly to the balance of yin and yang energetic forces (see Chapter 1). Rectangular or square shapes with their rigid angles have masculine yang qualities, while circles, ovals, and amorphous shapes have fluid, feminine, yin qualities. The octagon is a very auspicious Feng Shui shape because it duplicates the Bagua. Don't think in terms of bad shapes just inauspicious ones. Shapes with significant missing areas such as "u" or horseshoe forms are in this category.

✔ **Balance the colors in a sign according to the Five Elements.** Choose colors corresponding to the type of energy you want people to connect with your business. Blue is a color for clear, user-friendly communication; red — a yang color — suggests vital, active energy, whereas brown or earth tones suggest a calmer, more relaxed message.

✔ **Have your sign clearly lettered with a legible company logo.** See "Looking into logos," earlier in the chapter for more on logos. Ever drive by a sign and think, "What in heck was that?" and turn to take another look, thereby causing a three-car pileup? Bad Feng Shui. Bad, bad Feng Shui.

✔ **Make sure that the sign isn't confusing.** A sign with good Feng Shui is not cluttered or distracting. A good sign shouldn't be like one of those visual puzzles where you have to stand in front of it for ten minutes developing a blinding headache before saying, "I see the ship, Martha! Do you see the ship?"

✔ **Be sure the sign is legible from a passing car (if it faces a street).** A client or customer approaching your building should be able to find your business easily. Remember, you're in business. You WANT people to find you.

See Figure 7-7 for an example of a well-designed sign. Using a natural material, like the stone pictured below, is good Feng Shui. The company's name is legible and can be clearly seen from the street where the sign is placed. The blue logo symbolizes clear communication and the sign's area is neat and clean. Spotlights are in place to illuminate the sign so it can also be seen at night.

Placing and maintaining

Now that you've created your sign, consider location and maintenance.

✔ **Place your sign at a right angle to the building.** This placement, especially along a busy street, can catch the attention of potential customers. Vertical signs are eye-catching.

✔ **Be sure that a directory is readily available in the lobby.** Especially if you share office space with other companies.

✔ **Place a nameplate on the outside of the building.** It should list tenants. This helps reassure clients that they've found the correct building. Signs should also direct people to the correct place they want to find: Accounting and Administration, for instance.

✔ **Keep all signs clean and in good repair.** Repair a broken sign immediately. (Imagine the image a broken sign projects to potential customers!) The same goes for neon signs with no neon, or lighted signs with burned-out bulbs.

Figure 7-7: Well-designed sign.

Planning a Specific Business

After choosing a location and a logo, turn your attention to the building itself. An irregularly shaped building or shop is missing part of the Bagua, which is not auspicious. Choosing a more regular shape for the structure enhances your good fortune because all areas of the Bagua are represented and complete. But other Feng Shui considerations vary depending on the type of business you're conducting.

Retail stores and shops: Bringing in customers

The goal is to get good chi to flow easily and gently throughout the store — not in a direct arrow-line from front to back that makes the chi rush out the door. Your goal is to convince the chi to make a leisurely visit to your business, but you also want to encourage it to leave in a timely manner so it doesn't get trapped and create stagnant chi.

✔ **Make the main entrance easy to find.** Signs need to clearly direct customers to entrances and exits, and to various important points throughout the facility.

✔ **Use shorter furniture.** Don't block chi with tall shelves or other very high furniture. Such shelves can appear top-heavy and give customers an uncomfortable feeling. See the "Display spaces get attention" sidebar in this chapter for more information on merchandising.

✔ **Decorate the interior with your goals in mind.** If you want customers to have shorter visits, a slightly more yang décor may be called for. For example, at the local convenience store, where lots of people pop in to pick up a newspaper and pay for their gas, you don't necessarily want to encourage people to linger.

✔ **Consider incorporating the color red into your shop.** Red is the most powerful yang hue and is auspicious for retail enterprises. Hang signs from red string, use red paint to draw attention to special merchandise, letter signs in red.

✔ **Watch your red.** Don't paint the walls red — too much yang energy makes customers feel nervous and they don't linger. Usually, the longer a customer browses, the more money she spends. Consider adding a deeper hue such as a shade of burgundy to one wall to take advantage of the special energy of red without driving customers away.

✔ **Circular racks with hanging items (as in a clothing store) can be a more favorable way to arrange merchandise than stacking it on open shelves.**

✔ **A friendly sign can counteract the negativity of a locked display case.** Locked cases prevent theft, but they also mean the customer can't touch an item, which is essential to purchasing it.

✔ **Place the cash register carefully.** Putting it near the front entrance but not directly opposite the door is favorable. A mirror behind the cash register symbolically doubles the money. Don't place the register so it faces the front entrance directly. It also shouldn't face a toilet or kitchen where chi symbolically drains away.

Service establishments: Combining friendliness and function

Service businesses include restaurants, contractors, and many other types of establishments. For the sake of simplicity, we divided service businesses into businesses that serve customers on-site and businesses that provide their services elsewhere. The needs and functions of the two are slightly different.

Display spaces get attention

Although display spaces are primarily for retail shops, remember that any business can be on display in any number of ways, from the newspaper ad to the foyer. In all cases, it's a big help to use Feng Shui to create a favorable impression and to bring good fortune.

The front window of a shop can make a passer-by stop and then come in. Needless to say, the front window should be clean and kept free of posters and handbills. Put your best products in the window, arranged in a pleasing manner. Avoid clutter by not piling the display with widgets in every color you stock. Alternatively, spotlight one great item against a rich backdrop.

Serving customers off site

In this type of service business, employees go out into clients' homes and businesses or meet them at alternate sites. When clients don't come to your business, the premises should suit the needs of employees, allowing them to get their work done comfortably and happily.

Focus on applying Feng Shui principles that allow the free flow of chi. Chapters 2 and 3 provide details on how to design a workspace conducive to productivity. Chapter 12 talks about Feng Shui and places that aren't permanent.

Serving customers on site

When clients and customers come to your site, specific attention to their needs increases your chances of success.

Again, first impressions are important. Keep the place clean and well lighted. Mirrors symbolically double the number of customers, camouflage problem areas, and deflect cutting chi. They also magnify light. Determine whether you need more yin or more yang color. For instance, bright yang colors can be good for restaurants because they keep customers moving along, making room for new clients. Red can be good.

Chapter 8

Squaring Off with Cubicles

· ·

In This Chapter

▶ Learning to accept your cubicle

▶ Fixing a few cube problems

▶ Applying Feng Shui principles to your desk

· ·

Cubicles are one of the most popular methods of housing workers, except among those who have to sit in them. Although
some companies have tried different approaches to saving space
(such as the open concept office, described further in Chapter 9),
the cubicle in all its unlovely glory is here to stay.

You probably don't need us to tell you that a cubicle is a workspace in a larger office area, partitioned on three or four sides,
with an opening in one of the walls for an entrance. The walls of
the cubicle rarely reach the ceiling and the space the cubicle
encloses is often small. And don't forget the bland, neutral-colored
fabric that usually covers the cubicle walls. No wonder people con-
fined to cubicles feel like they've been sentenced to a padded cell
or have taken vows at the local monastery!

In this chapter, we show you how to Feng Shui those partitioned workspaces. Even in these limited areas — with all their
drawbacks — applying the principles of Feng Shui makes your environment more harmonious and comforting. You never know — you
may even begin to love those prison-gray burlap walls!

We also show you how to Feng Shui your desk, so that you can feel
good about your work environment even if your desk is all you have.
(No space is too small for the Feng Shui treatment!) The information
we provide about desks can be used whether your desk lives in a
cubicle, in a traditional office, or in an open concept office.

Although we use the word *desk*, most of the information we provide can be applied to any work surface, whether it's a countertop
or the living room table.

Loving Your Bland Burlap Walls

No one would ever accuse cubicle designers of creating beauty where none existed before — efficiency and getting the job done is considered more important than feeling good in the space. Creating beauty and aesthetics is your job. It may not seem possible at first glance, but you *can* turn that impersonal box into a welcoming, comfortable place to make your career aspirations come true. (And when *you're* the boss, you can ban those burlap walls!)

In order to apply the principles of Feng Shui to your cubicle, you need to take a realistic look around. With Feng Shui eyes you need to see it as it actually *is*. How big is it? What furniture and equipment do you have in it? (And what furniture and equipment do you actually need in it?) Before you can determine the cure, you have to know what the problem is.

But seeing your cubicle realistically isn't only a matter of measuring the area of the floor. Part of seeing the cubicle realistically is realizing how you *feel* about it — tapping into your intuition to find creative ways of solving design challenges and problems. If the burlap walls really don't bug you at all, then you can turn your attention to solving the problems that do bother you or make you feel uncomfortable. Chapter 1 talks about getting in touch with your gut feelings.

Feeling Like a Boob in Your Cube?

Cubicles have some drawbacks. Okay, cubicles have *many* drawbacks. But only some of them matter on an energetic, Feng Shui level. For one thing, you probably don't work at a desk in a cubicle; you have a counter. (In Feng Shui, it is more favorable to have a real desk for a feeling of stability and additional levels of confidence.) Storage units above and below the counter can limit your ability to move your work surface and your chair (making it difficult to face your most favorable direction — or even to see the entrance to your cube). The chances of your chair already facing your best direction are pretty slim, because the designer who laid out the office floor plan didn't take that into consideration. Even so, Feng Shui can cure that problem. See Figure 8-1 for an example of a well-designed working area. The walls don't reach the ceiling, allowing for flexibility. The curving wall in the foreground guides chi to the work area and the sliding screens allow access and provide privacy.

Figure 8-1: A Feng Shui–friendly working environment.

Peekaboo!

Your back probably faces your doorway. Otherwise, how could you work at your convenient countertop? But this is unfavorable in Feng Shui, which says that you should be able to see who's coming into your space and not be energetically distracted by people coming and going that you can't see.

Control the cube

Because you may have little control over the cubicle you're assigned — which direction the entrance faces, whether you have a desk or a countertop, whether you can move your desk or chair to a more auspicious direction, whether your cubicle is located next to the restroom — you may sometimes feel a little powerless. But as Feng Shui teaches, you are in control and have more power than you may believe. It may take a little brainstorming or creativity on your part, but you can do it!

No cubicle problem (not even orange burlap walls) is so great that Feng Shui cannot fix it. Remember to set every cure with intention, to achieve favorable results. Be energetic, be creative, and you can produce the positive energy needed to make your workspace attractive, welcoming, and comfortable.

Mirrors are "the aspirin of Feng Shui," because they're an easy cure for many energetic ills. Mainly, they serve to deflect negative chi and they're often placed outside above front doors to keep negative chi from entering a structure. They can also symbolically complete a space that is missing from the Bagua.

Try these cures if you cannot position your desk or chair to face the entrance:

- ✔ **Hang a mirror above your desk.** This helps you see the entrance and be aware of anyone coming into your space, which prevents surprises and distractions.

- ✔ **Prop a framed mirror on a stand.** Or use a makeup mirror that you can position accurately to reflect the entrance to your cubicle. (As Holly says, "Other people may think you're checking your makeup all day long, but they'll soon get over it.")

Multiplying by mirrors

Mirrors camouflage pillars and columns, which otherwise generate *sha chi,* or cutting chi. The use of mirrors can actually help make columns and square pillars visually disappear. Department stores and restaurants often use this design technique for expanding the vista of clients when they enter a space plagued by pillars or columns.

Any shape in a mirror is fine to use, too — if you need a mirror cure, any mirror is better than no mirror — but take the shape into consideration as you design your cubicle. Sharp edges may create cutting chi (described in depth in Chapter 2). An oval or round mirror might be a better choice if you already have an abundance of angular shapes within the space. Also pay attention to the frame of the mirror. A frame made of metal or wood can be used to help balance the Five Elements (discussed in Chapter 1). Select mirrors that show a true, undistorted reflection. Old, scratched or damaged mirrors do not work well as cures.

Cramping my chi

Because cubicles tend to be small, chi may flow either too quickly or very sluggishly. Chi should move through your cubicle in a gentle, smooth way. If your quarters seem quite cramped, a mirror on the wall helps visually enlarge the space. You can also place a mirror, especially an octagonal one, flat on your desktop and put on it a lovely object — perhaps a statue — to enhance the object and raise the chi in that Life Sector. (Turn to Chapter 3 for more information on the Bagua and the importance of Life Sectors.)

To counteract the smallness of the space, add

- ✔ **Mirrors.**
- ✔ **Bright colors.** Chapter 4 has more on color and texture.
- ✔ **Landscape pictures.**
- ✔ **A pony.** Oh wait, that will probably just make your cubicle *more* crowded!
- ✔ **Good lighting.** See Chapter 4 for more on lighting, too.

Also, make certain that nothing blocks the chi from flowing into the entrance to your cubicle. If something outside your cubicle interferes with the flow of chi, see whether you can get permission to move it. If you can't, encourage the movement of positive chi through cures. See Chapter 2 for more on chi and helping it along smoothly.

Cubicles do have an advantage over some other workspaces in that they are almost always of regular shape, either a square or a rectangle. This means that all sectors of the Bagua are included, and you don't have to find a cure for a missing Life Sector. We knew we could find something good to say about cubicles! However, if you do happen to have an oddly shaped cubicle, remember that you can use mirrors and crystals to replace missing Life Sectors.

Taking it down a decibel

You can't close the door when the outside world gets too loud: You don't have a door! Depending on where your cubicle is located in the office and who else is around you, volume control may be one of your biggest headaches.

Other than shouting, "Keep it down!" when the party around the water cooler gets going too loudly, what can you do?

✔ **Position yourself so that your desk or work surface is as far from the entrance to your cubicle as possible.** This helps protect you from noise outside your cubicle and allows you to see your space and who is coming into it.

✔ **Add plants to help absorb the sound.**

✔ **A nice water feature not only creates good energy, but it can help cover up some of the noise.** And if you add an aquarium you can complain to your fish when things get too loud in the outside world.

✔ **A tape player or radio with classical music playing softly can help camouflage extraneous noise and allow you to focus on getting your job done.** Think about using head-phones so you don't create noise for others.

See Chapters 4 and 6 for more information on keeping the volume turned low.

Tripping the fantastic light

If you work in a cubicle you may rarely see the sun. Only a lucky, lucky few get a cube with a window. Tiny, enclosed cubicles can seem dingy and dark. Lights help, of course, but add bright colors (rather than dark ones) as well as mirrors and crystals to make the place seem happier and more welcoming.

How else can you help fix this problem?

✔ **At the minimum, spend a few minutes outside each work-day.** Check out Chapter 4 for further information on lighting choices, such as full-spectrum lights that provide lighting similar to natural lighting.

✔ **Make sure you have adequate task lighting in your area.** If you don't have adequate overhead lighting, which can happen when cubicles are added to nooks and crannies of an office building, add floor lamps and uplights.

Chilling next to the water cooler

You probably don't have much choice about your cube's location. No one asked whether you minded sharing a wall with the bathroom. No one asked whether you wanted the water cooler to sit just outside the entrance. So what do you do if your cubicle doesn't just face an unfavorable direction, but is actually *in* an unfavorable position?

✔ **Hang a crystal near the entrance to your cubicle.** Don't bump your head on it, though — put it slightly to the side or actually inside your cubicle if you have to.

✔ **A wind chime works.** Unless a constant breeze flows through the office, the chime shouldn't bother your office mates at all.

✔ **A small water feature near the entrance can generate some positive chi.** Get a tiny waterfall going in there.

Chapters 1 and 7 describe the best locations for workspaces, depending on what your job is. If you're stuck in a stinky location (near the bathroom, perhaps?), Chapter 13 gives more cures.

Counteracting the countertop

By creating your workspace with intention, you can turn even the smallest, dingiest cubicle into a pleasant place to work. We know you're saying, "Yeah, right." But we mean it. By planning how you want to place objects — your desk, your equipment, other furniture — you can create powerful, positive energy in your cubicle (and even in yourself), energy that may translate into greater productivity and better satisfaction with your job.

Placing a template of the Bagua over a layout of your cubicle can help you decide where to place your desk (or where to place your chair and your work surface if you have only counters in your cubicle). Applying the Bagua also helps you see if you have inadvertently created a less-than-favorable situation (such as by putting your wastebasket in the Wealth sector). Because the north is the sector having to do with career, it's favorable to place your desk (or your chair and work surface) in this area. Chapter 3 talks about the Bagua in depth.

You can stimulate certain sectors of the Bagua to help solve problems you may be having in your working life. For example, if you're having trouble getting along with some co-workers, adding a plant, a crystal, or a lamp to the southwestern sector stimulates the chi and creates more positive energy in the Relationship Sector or in the northwest for Helpful People. The result is a better working relationship with those people you've been having difficulty with. Or just stop stealing their sodas out of the communal fridge!

If you're lucky enough to have a choice in your cell, uh cubicle, you may want to scan the following list for advice:

✓ **Choose the cubicle with the desk.** Working at a desk rather than a counter is generally more favorable.

✓ **Choose a cube entrance facing the south or one of your best directions.** (See Chapter 1 to determine your most favorable direction.)

✓ **Place your desk or chair so that it faces the entrance to your area but is not directly in front of the door or entrance.**

✓ **Choose a cubicle with four walls, a door, and some windows.** Wouldn't that be nice?

✓ **Place your desk or chair so that you face your favorable direction.** If you have to choose one or the other — either facing the entrance or facing your favorable direction — choose facing the entrance.

✓ **Create an arrangement of the desk and other furnishings that allows you to see as much of your cubicle or workspace as possible.** This can give you a feeling of more control over your space.

✓ **Place your desk so that it is as far from the entrance as possible.** Otherwise, you may feel distracted by people walking nearby.

✓ **Keep your desk out of the direct path from the entrance to your cubicle.** Instead of chi (and visitors) coming directly at you, it (and they) will flow gently and smoothly throughout your cubicle.

✓ **Eliminate large and bulky pieces of furniture and equipment.** Most cubicles are small, and large objects can make you feel small and overwhelmed.

✓ **Be sure your chair has more than adequate turn around space.**

✓ **Keep your desk away from a wall, allowing space on all sides.** Being able to get to your desk from different sides makes you feel more flexible and may help you feel safer (you have a way to "escape" if you need to and your own chi is not blocked).

In Figure 8-2 the desk faces a wall, while at the same time being much too close to each of the two doors opening into the office. It should be farther away from the doors for better placement.

People who have worked in your cubicle or at your desk previously may have left something behind besides that lingering odor of Old Spice, and that really old orange; something called *predecessor energy.* If the person ahead of you was promoted, the energy tends to be good, positive energy, and you may benefit from it. If the person was fired, left under unhappy circumstances, or was seriously ill you may have to deal with leftover negative energy. You may want to create some positive energy to counteract this residual negative predecessor energy. In Chapter 14, we give some tips on how to accomplish exactly that.

Figure 8-2: This inauspicious desk placement could lead to trouble.

Good doggie

Jennifer's big ole Alaskan Malamute Dakota insists on lying on the floor directly behind her chair, resulting in the occasional mashed tail and hurt feelings. Unfortunately, no Feng Shui cure exists for stubborn dogs, although she is frequently tempted to hang wind chimes from Dakota's collar. When Jennifer knows she will be moving around a lot in her workspace, she has to either evict Dakota or give her a chew toy in another corner of the room.

Size does matter: Does your desk measure up?

In traditional Feng Shui, masters feel that certain measurements or dimensions bring good luck whereas other dimensions are not so fortunate. According to traditional schools of Feng Shui, making sure that desks, chairs, windows, doors, and other objects have favorable measurements results in greater business success.

These measurements are based on dividing the diagonal of a square Chinese foot (which equals about 17 inches) into eight equal sections. The dimensions correspond with Eastern ideas of proportion in architecture called the *Divine Proportion*. The resulting "Feng Shui Ruler" can be applied to any type of furniture found in a workspace. The height, width, and length of a desk, according to this theory, should measure auspiciously. If the dimensions of a desk are unfavorable, choose a different desk.

Favorable:

0 to 2⅛ inches

Unfavorable:

From 2⅛ to 6⅜.

Favorable:

The next 4¼ inches: 6⅜ to 10⅝

The cycle continues in this way, with each additional 4¼ inches alternating between unfavorable and favorable. Thus, a desk that is 30 inches wide has unfavorable dimensions, whereas a desk that is 32 inches wide has favorable dimensions.

Other aspects of dimension are important in this theory. For example, it is favorable for an executive's desk to be larger than a subordinate's desk. In the same way, the executive's chair — and symbolically, the executive — is more powerful if it is larger than the visitor's chair. These proportions help shape the personal energetic power your surroundings create.

Sizing Up Your Desk

Organizing is especially important in a cubicle, because the space tends to be small and easily overwhelmed with clutter. Use your Feng Shui eyes to see what your cubicle looks like.

If you have reams of paper tacked to the walls, with each sheet bearing important information, you're creating visual clutter that may one day give you a migraine. Instead of using your walls like a bulletin board, file this information in relevant folders in your file cabinet. Jot down important addresses and phone numbers in the front of your Rolodex or flag them in the address book you use in your computer. Place guidelines you refer to often in one of your desk drawers rather than on the wall. Chapter 2 touches on organizing principles for workspaces.

You may have to make do with the desk that your boss assigns to you, but if you have a choice, choose the most favorable desk for the type of work you do. Take a look at Table 8-1 for more information.

Table 8-1	Desks and What You Do
What you do	*Favorable desk shape*
Concerned with making money; in sales or finance	A strong shape, such as a rectangle.
Creative type or working in marketing	Curved, kidney-shaped, oval, or round desks. Round desks may discourage people from sitting at them for very long, however.
Bruise your hip on the desk corners a lot	A rectangular desk with rounded corners prevents negative chi (and also prevents you from bruising your hip on the corner of your desk!).

Other things come into play as well. Table 8-2 gives the scoop.

Can the notes

Jennifer used to attach sticky notes to the frame of her computer monitor so she wouldn't forget to do what needed to be done. Holly and Feng Shui convinced her that this was needless clutter, and now she keeps a pretty notebook on her desk and jots "to do" items in it as she becomes aware of them. This is certainly more attractive than yellow pieces of paper fluttering in the air, and it lets her concentrate on what she is doing right now instead of being distracted by the other things that also need to be done.

Table 8-2   The Good, the Less-than-Good, and the Why

Less auspicious desks	Why	Good desks
L-shaped and other irregularly shaped desks	Some part of the Bagua is missing. Irregular shapes can seem less solid and symbolically cut off communication between the worker sitting behind it and her co-workers and boss.	Get a solid-shaped desk.
Black desks, high-contrast desks or desks with highly polished surfaces	May make it difficult for you to concentrate and do your work. The glare from them may slow you down.	Wooden desks are more favorable than metal desks.
Glass-top desks	May let projects, ideas, and money symbolically slip through your hands. Plus staring at the floor can be distracting when you should be focusing on your work.	Choose a desk with a plain surface that doesn't distract you.
Desk substitutes, like tables or countertops.	Desks with only a top and legs can make you feel vulnerable.	A front panel on your desk (sometimes called a privacy screen) can make you feel stronger and more powerful. Front and side panels that reach all the way to the floor are more protective than panels that reach only partway.

A solid desk is more favorable than a flimsy one, for reasons that are probably obvious. Not only is a flimsy desk frustrating to work at (not unlike trying to eat from a wobbly table), but symbolically you're also expressing or communicating weakness, not strength. Same goes for your desk chair. A solid chair gives you support and strength; a weak, squeaky, or wobbly chair may make you feel vulnerable and unstable.

Using the Bagua on your desktop

No, we mean using the Bagua on top of your desk, not your desktop computer! (Although you can apply the Bagua to your computer, too, if you want.) The Bagua can be applied to your desktop to help you enhance your career success.

Consciously choose what you want to place in each area of the Bagua. Don't let unopened mail sit in the Marriage/Relationships sector if you know having a photograph of you and your significant other in that area is more favorable. See Figure 8-3 for an example of Feng Shui principles in action on a desktop. The phone is in the Wealth sector, which encourages business. The green plant in the Family sector may improve relationships with coworkers. Green is this section's associated color, and plants raise chi. The fu dogs in the middle of the desk are red, the right color for the Fame sector. The photo of the kid in the Children sector raises chi and also reminds the worker that he has a life outside work. And the black appointment book in the Career sector enhances chi and encourages orderliness.

To place the Bagua, remember that your desk's "entrance" is where you sit facing your desk in your chair. Put the Career sector here, and see where the other sectors fall on your desk.

Figure 8-3: Lots of goodies here make for success.

Auspicious placements on your desk include

✔ **Placing your phone in the Wealth sector.** Doing so symbolizes more people calling for your business.

✔ **Arranging a light in the Fame sector.** This brightens your prospects for becoming well known for what you do or for improving your reputation in your company.

✔ **Setting a plant in the Family sector.** This helps create peaceful relationships with others.

✔ **Putting a cure in the Children sector — a bell, crystal, or mirror.** Doing so can help improve communication with others.

✔ **Using the appropriate color in its related sector.** Good energy is on its way in this case. Black or deep blue in the Career sector may improve your career success; red in the Fame sector can improve your reputation; and purple in the Wealth sector can improve your finances.

You don't have to see the cures for them to be beneficial. You simply have to *place them with intention.* Putting a mirror in the desk drawer that corresponds to a sector can work as well as putting a mirror on the surface of your desk. (If no desk drawer is available, tape or secure the cure to the underside of your desktop or countertop.) See Chapter 1 for more information on placing with intention.

Just as it is most favorable to keep a balance of the Five Elements in your workspace as a whole, it is helpful to keep the Elements balanced on your desk, as well. See Chapters 1 and 4 for more information on balancing this Feng Shui basic principle.

As you apply the Five Elements to your desktop, remember that colors, shapes, and objects symbolize them. You can strengthen the elements by placing them in their corresponding sector of the Bagua. For example, because the Fame sector is associated with Fire, placing a red object in that sector enhances the Fire element *and* stimulates the Fame sector. Lights, candles, and sunlight symbolize fire, so a lamp or decorative candle in the Fame sector does the same work as a red object.

Chapter 9

Grasping the Open Concept Office

*I*n *open concept* or *open plan* offices, workers share one extensive work area that has few interior walls and no traditional personal offices (except maybe the CEO's office). Open concept offices don't use screens or partitions to separate one person's workspace from another's.

These offices are often designed for a high-tech look, boasting high ceilings and exposed beams and ductwork intended to make them seem open and airy. Although the stated purpose of these types of office spaces is to facilitate communication and networking among employees, workers in open concept offices may feel vulnerable and energetically threatened by the lack of personal space and boundaries.

Open concept offices have particular Feng Shui challenges. If you can remember the challenges you faced as a kid in the classroom, you can visualize some of the challenges you may encounter as a worker in an open concept office (not least that it's more interesting to gossip with Jimmy than to do your math). In this chapter, we show you cures for some of these problems.

> ## Why open that can of worms?
>
> Some companies prefer these types of offices because they feel it improves communication among employees and levels out the corporate hierarchy. After all, if the boss is just across the way sitting at a desk that looks just like yours, she seems a lot more accessible, right? And if you need to ask Joe for some numbers to crunch, it's a lot easier to call over to the next desk than it is to leave your cubicle, get on the elevator to the fifteenth floor, find Joe's cubicle and pick up the numbers. In addition, open concept offices allow a certain amount of flexibility. You just hired four new workers? Shove the old workers a little closer together and add a couple more desks. No need to find more office space or to add a new wing onto the building; simply consolidate your workers into one area.

You Weren't Raised in a Barn but You Work in One

Unfair as the comparison may be, an open concept office is a lot like a barn — only at least a barn has stalls. Open concept offices don't generally provide barriers such as interior walls or partitions — in short, they offer no privacy and no way to keep distractions out.

But the same problems that you find in a barn, you find in an open concept office — lack of privacy, lots of noise, plenty of distractions.

Although the lack of barriers helps keep chi flowing smoothly throughout the space, the noise and disruptions that characterize open concept offices run counter to Feng Shui principles. Still, open concept offices are not without promise. You *can* make them more comfortable, inviting, and attractive, even if you can't talk your boss into putting up some nice cubicles. Using some of the principles of Feng Shui and some common cures, you can make an open concept office pleasant and welcoming — you may even learn to *enjoy* working in a barn.

Applying the Principles

In an open concept office, you apply the principles of Feng Shui just as you do in any other workspace. You may be able to stake out a claim on a few feet of ground beyond your desk and apply the principles of Feng Shui to a few square yards of real estate surrounding you. If not, then apply them to your desktop. For more details on desktop arrangement see Chapter 8.

Allow the chi to flow smoothly, apply the Bagua to your workspace, balance yin and yang qualities, and include representations of each of the Five Elements, as we describe in Chapters 1 and 2. Setting intentions as you place objects and design cures is crucial to successfully creating the type of energy you want to create. Keep in mind that passive, yin energy can be created by using dark colors and rounded shapes, whereas active, yang energy can be created by using bright colors and square, rectangular, or angular shapes.

Almost all offices have more yang than yin energy, which comes from all those people doing all that work. Busy, busy, busy! Open concept offices may create even more yang energy, especially if the furnishings are arranged so chi moves too quickly. Open concept offices may also be loud — and even chaotic.

The yang energy may become too out of balance with the yin energy and may create tension, frustration, and loss of productivity among workers. Chapter 1 describes creating balance between yin and yang energy in more detail.

Yin energy can be introduced by using darker colors, by taking advantage of noise-reducing objects and practices, and by carefully arranging the desks and other furnishings. But don't slow the chi so much that it stagnates. Instead, find a balance so that chi can move smoothly throughout the entire work area.

When possible, enlist the help of the other workers and your boss to keep the chi flowing throughout the open concept office. Raising the chi in the entire area requires more than just your individual efforts (although your individual efforts will be very meaningful even if no one else buys into the Feng Shui way). Encourage the boss to arrange furniture so that chi flows smoothly and gently throughout the area. Take responsibility for reducing clutter in the office yourself and show others how they can pitch in and help.

The drawbacks to an open concept office are almost always quite apparent to the powers-that-be, although they may not like to admit it; so if you can show them how to temper some of the problems using Feng Shui principles, they may be happy to listen to your suggestions. See Figure 9-1 for an example of an open concept office. In this illustration, the small barriers between each desk help give each worker some privacy and cut down on noise. The desk areas are neat and clutter-free. Because the workers' backs are to the traffic flow, placing mirrors above their desks would help them see who's coming. Placing trash bins under the desks (or at least concealing them) would also improve Feng Shui.

Figure 9-1: Open concept office.

Reducing the roar of the crowd

The lack of barriers in open concept offices means that noise travels everywhere. High ceilings allow sound to echo throughout the space. And because you have no convenient office door to shut out that noise, you have to live with it. This can be a particular problem if people do a lot of talking, either on the phone or with colleagues. Not only do high ceilings allow sound to echo throughout, but on an energetic level, they can also make you feel very exposed and vulnerable.

These cures can help:

- ✔ **Play soft classical music.** This helps reduce the distraction of other noise and can camouflage the loud conversation your co-workers are having across the way.

- ✔ **Create a sense of being grounded and protected in your workspace.** Have your back to a wall, for example, for the feeling of stability and support this gives you.

✔ **Emphasize the Earth, Fire and Metal elements in your work area.** These three elements are connected and can make you feel more grounded and stable. Use a few growing plants in ceramic containers, and emphasize yellow and earth tone colors to add Earth. Add a red or flame-shaped object and a few brass picture frames to incorporate Fire and Metal.

✔ **Use a small cure such as a mirror or crystal.** These objects symbolize the water element, and the Water element balances the Earth element. An actual water element such as a simple desktop fountain on your desk or nearby surface can also be used. Sorry, the coffee maker right next to your desk doesn't count!

Reducing the noise in an open concept office also requires you to enlist the help of others, including fellow workers and the boss. Make it a priority to gently convince others to be respectful of the need for quiet so that everyone can concentrate on getting work done. See Chapters 4 and 6 for more information on reducing noise in workspaces.

Beaming you up

Overhead beams, sometimes used for structural reasons and sometimes for decorative reasons, also create oppressive, weighty energy. Exposed ductwork, which in other buildings is hidden by ceilings, is left in plain sight in open concept offices. Ductwork may look cool but it interrupts the flow of chi.

Get rid of that ductwork if you can, but in most cases this is impossible. A few cures are available to help counteract the oppressive effect of ceiling beams and exposed ductwork.

✔ **Attach false ceilings to beams.** This is usually not practical for workspaces (unless you own the company and don't mind spending the money).

✔ **Mirror the beams.** This is a tricky cure and may be expensive.

✔ **Move your desk so you're not seated directly under a beam.** If beams or exposed ductwork hang directly above your desk, you may feel depressed and uninspired in your work. (You may feel this way even if you're not seated directly under a beam, but that's another problem entirely.) Arrange other furniture so that guests aren't seated directly under beams, either.

✔ **Hang bamboo flutes facing each other diagonally on the beam.** This traditional cure raises the chi and removes the energetic weight of the beam. No, you don't have to play the flute for this cure to work.

✔ **Paint the beams and ductwork a lighter color.** The energy they produce is less oppressive. Covering beams with material, such as muslin, is also effective, but this material can collect dust, creating negative chi.

✔ **Install uplights.** They visually counteract the weighing-down effect of beams and exposed ductwork.

See Chapter 4 for additional cures for this problem, including traditional Chinese cures.

Minding your own beeswax

Because open concept offices don't have screens, walls, or partitions, you can see what everyone else is doing (and vice versa). You may become distracted from your own work. This can be a particularly troublesome challenge at those times when your own work is not especially fascinating.

One of the challenges of open concept offices is to create a feeling of privacy while you're working. This can be especially important if you make sensitive phone calls, meet with clients, or otherwise conduct business that you don't want everyone to overhear. Try creating symbolic barriers that set boundaries around your workspace. And because you're still in the same room with them, the advantages of the open concept office — networking and interaction with colleagues — are not lost.

 Face your desk away from the interior of the work area (but not so that your back is to the entrance to your own personal workspace). If you're not in a good position to see the other workers, you're more likely to keep your mind on the work in front of you.

 Try these tricks:

✔ Noise-canceling earphones on your head.

✔ A low screen near the side of your desk.

✔ A visitor's chair, placed to the front or the side of your desk.

✔ A tall tree-like plant near your desk.

✔ A gorgeous plant or two near the edge of your desk.

✔ A few photographs across the front of your desk.

✔ A row of reference books sandwiched between two attractive bookends resting on the front or side of your desk.

✔ A simple throw rug on the floor can define your space.

✔ A low file cabinet positioned next to your desk can act as a boundary.

Calling Ed Asner: Desks Together Newsroom Style

Unfortunately for everyone's chi, desks and workstations are often tossed together practically at random in open concept offices. And when little attention is paid to placement, chi can move too rapidly through an office or can collect and stagnate. Either can be unpleasant for the people who have to work in the office.

Certain furniture arrangements are more favorable than others: Desks lined up in rows allow chi to flow smoothly and gently through and among them. Desks that face each other directly may feel some confrontational energy. It is better to have desks side by side (more collaborative and companionable). Having wide aisles between rows of desks allows people and chi to move freely. In other words, arrange the desks in a regular, simple way.

Avoid irregularly shaped arrangements of desks. T-shaped or L-shaped furniture arrangements can prevent chi from moving freely throughout the office. If possible, the office entrance should not open directly onto one of the desks. Corners and angles can be softened with plants, which can also serve to mark boundaries of individual workspaces and provide privacy. Chapter 2 talks more about softening angles for chi's sake.

See Figure 9-2 for another example of an open concept office. In this photo, natural light from the skylight is good Feng Shui, and the comfortable, upholstered chairs make visitors feel welcome. You can see that screens and partitions have been added to help make workers feel more private. The rug in the center helps balance the brick and metal and symbolically creates a separate area. All this office needs is natural carpet throughout to further balance the brick and plants to soften the pillar.

Figure 9-2: Another open concept office.

Chapter 10

Tackling the Traditional Office

● ●

In This Chapter

▶ Finding the best layout for a traditional office

▶ Making a plan to remedy problems

● ●

*T*he traditional personal office seems to be in danger of extinction. You know — a workspace enclosed by four walls, with a functioning door used by a single worker. A place where you can shut the door and clear all the work off your desk with no interruptions, or even take a brief catnap with no one the wiser.

More and more companies are creating cubicles and open-concept offices (see Chapters 8 and 9), but we bet traditional offices will be around for a long time. Why? Because in Feng Shui traditional offices are about the most favorable type of workspace possible. They're usually regularly shaped, allow privacy, and symbolize a degree of personal power.

Although traditional offices will probably never completely replace those orange-burlap cubicles most people toil in, they'll always exist, and they'll always be something to aspire to. Unless that smarmy new hire gets there first.

In this chapter, we apply the principles of Feng Shui to a traditional office and the lucky person inhabiting that workspace. We show how Feng Shui can help you create more power and may even increase your chances of career success.

Kicking It in the Corner Office

In general, the most favorable office is square or rectangular, with a door facing either the worker's most favorable direction or south, and a window or two to let in natural light (it's best if the window actually opens). This ideal office is located at the center rear of the office building, a strong, supported position where powerful chi collects.

If you're in a multi-story building, being a few floors up can enhance your power, but being on the top floor can place you in a vulnerable position. Like standing on the highest hill during a thunderstorm, working at the top of a building can make you feel a little exposed. A floor partway up is more protected from natural and human catastrophes than a ground floor office or a penthouse suite. See Figure 10-1 for examples of traditional office layouts that allow the chi to flow freely throughout the workspace. These layouts are regular, and nothing about the arrangement of furnishings will cause chi to stick or stagnate.

Well, it's nice to dream, isn't it? Unless you're one of the lucky few, your office probably doesn't measure up to all those criteria. Never fear! You can still arrange it to create good energy that can help you achieve your career goals.

Getting Plans Down on Paper

To create favorable Feng Shui chi for your career, and a work setting that makes you feel comfortable and happy, you need a plan. And the plan starts with you looking at your office and seeing what's really there, not just what you hope will be there, like those six awards for selling the most widgets this quarter.

You may have to dig down a bit to actually see what your office looks like. In fact, clearing the clutter before you start is not only good Feng Shui, but it will help you focus on the next steps, such as curing floor plan problems and arranging your furniture in the most auspicious way.

To start, draw a simple layout of your office:

- ✔ Room shape
- ✔ Location of doors and windows
- ✔ Architectural features such as pillars and posts
- ✔ Position of furniture

See Figure 10-2 for a sample of an office plan.

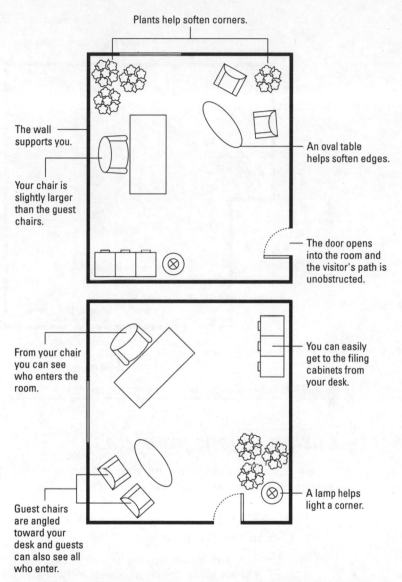

Plants help soften corners.

The wall supports you.

Your chair is slightly larger than the guest chairs.

An oval table helps soften edges.

The door opens into the room and the visitor's path is unobstructed.

From your chair you can see who enters the room.

You can easily get to the filing cabinets from your desk.

A lamp helps light a corner.

Guest chairs are angled toward your desk and guests can also see all who enter.

Figure 10-1: These traditional office layouts are just what the chi ordered.

Once you've got this down on paper, you can more easily visualize Feng Shui challenges, and you can start brainstorming for creative Feng Shui cures. Flip to the Appendix and you'll find some blank workspace sketchpads to use for your drawing.

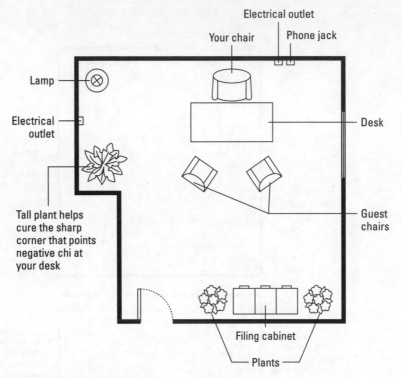

Figure 10-2: Drawing a plan for your office: You can do it!

Curing layout problems

Once you've drawn the layout for your office as it is, you can begin creating a more favorable workspace.

1. **Analyze the layout.**

2. **Plan how you're going to:**

   - **Cure any layout problems.** Use music, light, plants, mirrors, and crystals to raise the chi in areas that may need it, for instance. Types of layout plans that definately need attention include irregularly-shaped offices, offices with pillars or columns with square edges, and offices with windows directly opposite the door.

   - **Arrange furnishings auspiciously.** See "Moving the mauve furniture" later in this chapter for more details on how to do this.

   - **Allow for chi's free flow and find solutions for negative chi energy.** De-clutter the space (if you haven't done so already). Using your Feng Shui eyes, try to find any sources of negative or cutting chi, such as sharp edges pointing directly at you, and either eliminate the edges or camouflage them with plants, fabric, or doors.

- **Balance the Five Elements.** Remember, color, shape and material are all associated with each of the elements. If you need to add Fire to your space, you can add a red accent, a flame-shaped object, or a light source to your space.

- **Keep yin and yang energy in equilibrium.** Because workspaces tend to produce more yang energy by their very function, you may need to add yin versions of colors to your space to keep the energy in balance. For example, you can use burgundy instead of bright red to symbolize the Fire element. The burgundy is a more yin color than bright red.

3. **Follow your plan and achieve lasting happiness and business success.**

   And never lose your favorite pen again!

See Figure 10-3 for an example of a well-designed office. The chair faces the door and is set back. The closed shelves above the computer prevent cutting chi. This office is squeaky clean and organized — no clutter here! The rounded desk for conferences encourages brainstorming and discourages time-wasting activities. However, Feng Shui elements could be applied to the desktop to make things even better. The stairs could pose a problem because chi may go directly down the staircase.

Bagua-ing the corner suite

Apply the Bagua to your office just as you apply it to any other space. If you have an irregularly-shaped office, the Bagua can show you which Life Sectors are missing, and you can enact a cure to symbolically complete those sections. The Bagua also shows you the most favorable positions for furniture and accessory placement. For example, it's unfavorable to place a wastebasket or a shredder in the Wealth Sector.

Place the Bagua over a layout of your office with the North side of the Bagua corresponding with the wall that contains the door to your office. This shows you how different areas of your office fall in the Bagua. See Chapter 8 for information on applying the Bagua to your desktop.

Figure 10-4 shows an office in need of some help. A wall supports the chair when you are at the desk. However, when you turn to work at the computer, your back is to the door, which is not good Feng Shui. A mirror over the computer would help. The phone should be on the desk so it can be answered easily. Task lighting on the desk would prevent eyestrain and clutter should be removed and organized. An enclosed cabinet or bookshelf for storage would prevent sha chi.

Figure 10-3: This is a well-designed office.

Moving the mauve furniture

To keep the chi flowing smoothly throughout your office, you need to do two things: get rid of the clutter and arrange your furnishings most favorably. When you arrange your furnishings, you can also use Feng Shui principles to create more personal power for yourself, which can enhance your career success.

Reduction of clutter is one of the key principles of Feng Shui. If you don't know what clutter is, take a look around. The pile of magazines that have been sitting in the corner for three years qualifies, as do the candy bar wrappers stuffed in your desk drawer. If you take a look around and don't see anything that qualifies, either you're oblivious and need a second opinion, or you can relax and move on to arranging your furniture auspiciously.

Figure 10-4: This office could use some help. Never fear! Feng Shui is here.

These tips can help control clutter

- ✔ Eliminate large, bulky pieces of furniture, especially if your area is small.

- ✔ Keep only those few pieces that you must have in your office, and that you use regularly.

- ✔ Use the Bagua to help you position your furniture favorably.

  - Place guest chairs in the Relationships/Marriage or Helpful People sector to improve your working relationships with people who come to visit you.

  - Hang your diploma and other credentials on the wall in the Fame sector to improve your reputation in your company.

Placing desk and guest chairs

The *power position,* the most favorable position, the one that creates the impression of strength and confidence, for your desk is facing the entrance to your office, in the corner farthest from the door, but not directly in front of the entrance. See Chapter 8 for more information on placing your desk and on applying the principles of Feng Shui to your desk.

Wishing for a window

Although it is more favorable to have a window that lets in sunlight and fresh air, if you don't have one in your office, all is not lost. You can

✔ Install full-spectrum lighting

✔ Get some daily exposure to the sun

✔ Install mirrors, look-alike windows with mirrors behind, or landscape pictures

If you do have a window in your office, especially a large window, sitting with your back to it can make you feel vulnerable and unsupported. You usually feel stronger and more protected if your back is to a wall. Chapter 4 talks more about windows and light.

Placing the desk slightly off to the side

✔ Allows you to see visitors as they enter your office, but keeps chi from hitting you directly as it enters the office.

✔ Feels less confrontational to many people.

✔ Allows chi to enter and circulate smoothly and freely.

✔ Keeps you from getting distracted by every person who passes by your door.

Your desk should

✔ Be placed so that you can easily get to it from any side. Well, it might be kind of hard to get to your chair from the front of your desk, but you know what we mean.

✔ Let you have your back to a wall while seated, pardner. (This is a strong, protected position.)

✔ Have plenty of room behind it so you don't keep banging your chair into the wall as you come and go.

✔ Allow your chair to slide in and out without hitting any obstructions. Placing a credenza or other worksurface behind you is common, but be sure that it does not crowd your movement or obstruct your chi.

Having all furnishings where you can see them from your desk is favorable. This keeps you from being taken by surprise.

To maintain this power position, arrange guest chairs so they

- ✔ Face your desk. Having their backs to the door makes guests feel slightly more vulnerable, which may or may not be what you want to achieve.

- ✔ Are to the side of your desk. That way visitors can also see the door.

In addition to placing guest chairs correctly, choosing their size is important.

- ✔ Guest chairs smaller than your chair gives you a slightly more powerful position.

- ✔ Chairs of equal size placed around a round or oval table are favorable for collaborative efforts.

Placing file cabinets, work tables, and more

When you place a piece of furniture, you're not just placing a functional object where you can have access to it. You're designing according to the principles of Feng Shui so consider the following:

- ✔ Consider the Life Sector it inhabits. While nothing is wrong with placing a credenza in the Fame sector, adding a nice lamp or pretty red vase to the top of the credenza helps stimulate chi in this area.

- ✔ Be sure work tables have adequate lighting nearby. Chapter 4 sheds some more light on that topic.

- ✔ Ensure that people can get into work tables without obstructions and that they're able to move around the table.

- ✔ Keep electronic equipment to a minimum in your office.

- ✔ Place the keyboard and monitor slightly to the side on your desk, this allows you to see visitors. See Chapter 6 for more information on electronic equipment.

See Figure 10-5 for an example of an auspicious arrangement of office furniture. Figure 10-6 might scare the Feng Shui right outta you.

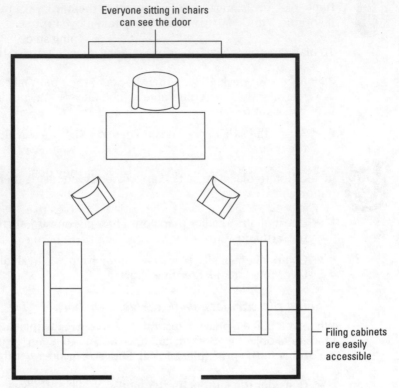

Figure 10-5: Arranging furniture and equipment in a pattern like this will benefit everyone.

Cutting chi off at the knees is bad

Allow the free flow of auspicious chi energy throughout your office. In general, keeping the center area free of obstructions and clutter helps promote the movement of chi.

The sharp angles and edges of much office furniture, such as filing cabinets and bookcases, can create *sha chi*, or cutting chi — especially when those angles are aimed directly at you. Chapter 2 has more information on avoiding negative chi.

To prevent the cutting chi from affecting you, try

✔ Not to sit with your back to a window. Doing so can make you feel vulnerable and unsupported.

✔ Taking down any object that hangs over your chair. Hanging objects such as plants, mobiles, and light fixtures can feel threatening.

✔ Moving your chair so that you don't sit directly under beams.

✔ Using furnishings with rounded corners whenever possible.

✔ Placing sharp edges and angles so that they don't point directly at you.

✔ Placing doors or glass fronts on bookshelves to eliminate visual clutter and prevent the contents from sending cutting chi. Harsh angles coming from corners or sharp edges of any furniture can be camouflaged with a trailing plant or a draped fabric.

✔ Placing furniture like file cabinets and credenzas against the walls.

✔ Adding plants, draped fabric, lovely objects with gentle lines, mirrors, and crystals. Chapters 4 and 5 talk about plants and fabric, respectively. Chapter 16 reveals more cure help.

✔ Putting lights, plants, mirrors and crystals in nooks and crannies.

✔ Arranging furnishings in semicircular patterns. This is good in a work area with more than one desk or an office with several pieces of large furniture. These pieces also ideally face the entrance.

✔ Positioning shared work areas or desks so that each employee has privacy and the ability to focus. Desks directly facing each other can be distracting.

You can raise the chi in all areas at the same time, or you can choose one or two areas to concentrate on. Any combination of cures and chi raising efforts can work in Feng Shui!

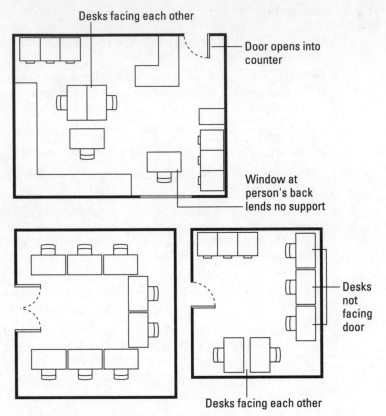

Figure 10-6: You want to stay far away from arrangements like these. They'll choke the chi right from your office.

Chapter 11

Jamming in Your PJs: Working from Home

In This Chapter

▶ Finding a place for your stuff

▶ Choosing the right furnishings

▶ Making your home office a success

S ome lucky people get to work in their pajamas at home. Ah, the freedom from the boss, the quiet that comes from being all by your lonesome — and the call of the refrigerator and the non-stop barking of your neighbor's dog.

Okay, having an office at home has its benefits and its drawbacks. In this chapter, we show you how to create a balanced, relaxed environment to work from at home. Applying the principles of Feng Shui is as important in your home office as it is in any workspace. Not only does it create a pleasant, welcoming environment, but it can also help you achieve your career goals — and you have goals, even if you don't shower before noon!

Whether you're a *telecommuter* — a corporate employee who occasionally works from the computer at home — or an entrepreneur building a multi-million dollar business in the spare bedroom, we give you valuable advice on how to apply the principles of Feng Shui to home workspaces.

Placing Your Workspace

Jennifer's desk used to face the toilet, and she wondered why she dreaded going to work every day. Once Holly convinced her to move her desk, she actually started to enjoy her job, and realized that editors aren't so bad after all.

Eating bonbons in the bathtub?

While working from home can be a pleasant change from the routine, it can also be quite distracting. If you're reconciling account statements in your cubicle at the bank, you don't notice that the carpet needs to be vacuumed and then wrestle with your conscience over whether you should do that now or wait until later (you're not being paid to vacuum!). You don't notice the dirty dishes piled in the sink and wonder whether you should do them now while you're thinking of it, or later after you've finished that report for your client (you're not being paid to do dishes!). But if you let home and personal distractions get in the way of doing your work, you'll be on your way to the unemployment office instead of the CEO's suite.

By applying the principles of Feng Shui, and setting your intentions as you do so (say something like, "I will ignore the pile of laundry in the bathroom while I'm working"), you can make your home workspace attractive and comfortable — a place where you want to work, and where you're able to tune out the distractions of everyday life.

We know you won't make that same mistake, but finding the right place for your home workspace requires more thought than just avoiding the ceramic bowl. In other words, you want to choose the most *auspicious* (favorable) location for your workspace to help you become and remain successful in your career.

We know, we know, your house or apartment or motor home doesn't necessarily give you lots of options about where to put your workspace. But the tips we give you in this section help you do the best you can with what you've got! First we show you how to choose the best location for your office, then how to deal with any floor plan challenges you may have, and finally explain how to furnish your home office the Feng Shui way.

Location, location, oh — and staplers

To determine where in your home you should place your office, make some decisions about your work. If you need natural lighting to paint your illustrations for children's books, then putting your studio in the underground basement won't work.

Follow this list to start plotting your office spot:

1. **Decide what you need in your workspace.**

   This depends, of course, on what you do in your workspace. If you're a clothing designer, you need space for your computer and a drafting table. You may also need space for fabric samples, a sewing machine and accessories, and a place for people to try on the clothes you've made.

2. **Make a list of what you use regularly in your workspace.**

   If you already work from home this is easy. If you don't already work from home, guess. This spare but complete list should include

   - Equipment
   - Furniture
   - Accessories

3. **Determine your most auspicious directions.**

   Turn to Chapter 1 to find out what this most favorable direction is. It is favorable if the entrance to your home office faces one of your auspicious directions.

4. **Find a good location for your new home office.**

   Locating your home office in the southwest sector is favorable, because this is the Wealth sector. Other favorable locations include the north, which is the Career sector and the northeast, which is the Knowledge sector.

   Try to find a space with these qualities:

   - Located in the center rear of your home
   - The door or entrance to the space is facing an auspicious direction
   - You aren't constantly confronted by the property of that one neighbor who never mows the lawn

   If you can't find a space with its entrance in one of your most favorable directions, try one that faces south. According to classical Feng Shui masters, south is usually a favorable direction for anyone. That's a much better choice than facing in an unfavorable direction!

No bedroom to spare

Sometimes people have a convenient spare bedroom or den they can turn into a home office. The spare room usually has enough space for your equipment, a door that closes, and a window. That's a Feng Shui trifecta! What more could you ask for?

But not everyone is so fortunate. If you don't have a trifecta, work with what you have. The beauty of Feng Shui is that it can help you turn almost any space into an attractive, welcoming niche! So be creative — while taking into consideration how much space you really need to do your job (in other words, trying to shove your photography studio into the hall closet doesn't work and just frustrates you).

Consider these options:

- ✔ **Can the basement or a portion of the basement be turned into a workspace?** This is a valid choice only if the basement isn't the type of place that grows three different kinds of mushrooms. Remember, you want to feel good about your work.

- ✔ **Can you use the attic if you put a floor down and some drywall up?** And don't forget to kick out the spiders, or at least ask them nicely to leave.

- ✔ **Can you convert the garage (or some portion of it) into a workspace without completely destroying your home's property value?** Or destroying your spouse's desire to keep every single item he finds on the street and stores it in the garage?

- ✔ **Can you screen off part of a larger room?** Placing bookshelves or screens across one end of a room can give you a separate workspace. This is an especially good choice if you have an odd-shaped living space, because creating two regular shaped rooms out of one odd-shaped room raises the chi!

- ✔ **Can a closet be turned into a mini-office?** By scooting a small desk in and adding shelves to the walls, many a walk-in closet has been converted into a reasonable workspace (especially for someone who doesn't do a lot of work at home).

- ✔ **Can you enclose a patio and turn it into a workspace?** In some areas of the country, an enclosed patio can be used year-round.

- ✔ **Can you add a room?** This may seem outrageously expensive at first, but some companies sell prefabricated rooms that you can easily attach to your house. Or, you can put a yurt in your backyard.

Bedrooms are for sleeping and for, umm, romance. By putting your computer in your bedroom, you're asking for trouble in the Relationship sector! (And while you're at it, get the TV out of there, too.)

Finagling with family

Family members are anyone you live with, whether they're actually related to you or not. (Saying, "Family members or other people you live with, whether you're related to them or not" throughout the whole chapter seems a little awkward.)

People resist change, so don't be surprised if a kid (possibly one of your own) objects when you take over the playroom to make it into your home office. To avoid conflict (Feng Shui is about finding and creating balance and pleasing design, not making everyone mad at you), follow these steps to help your family accept the changes that creating a home office involves:

- Get your family involved from the beginning. No one likes being told what's going to happen without getting a chance to express her opinion. Your children can help you brainstorm possible locations for your workspace. Your spouse can help you make the final decision.

- Once the process has started, keep them informed. Let them know that you've narrowed the choices down and you're going to use the playroom for your office. Don't just start moving your computer equipment in while they're trying to play Nintendo.

- Offer alternatives now that you've stolen the playroom from them. (It helps if you think of the alternatives in advance.) Tell them that you're going to finish the basement or build shelves for toys in the living room.

Creating room plans

You've found your spot, you've staked your claim. Now you have to figure out where to put the computer. Create a floor plan to help find the best places for your furniture, equipment, posable action figures, and accessories — and to help prevent you from creating Feng Shui problems. If your home workspace is a spare room, you can treat it like a traditional office; Chapter 10 tells you all about those. If you're using a space taken from another room, you have another meatball altogether, and that's what we tackle here.

Allow for the free, smooth movement of chi and for adequate storage. See "Fitting your room for the Bagua" in this chapter for more information on choosing favorable places for your furniture and equipment. See Chapter 3 for more information on drawing workspace layouts.

1. **If your office space has been carved out of the living room, draw the entire living room.**

   We're talking warts, pillars, windows and all.

2. **Indicate what part of the space you're using for your home office.**

   This helps develop a plan to

   - Separate the two areas without interfering with the flow of chi.

   - Anticipate problems you may cause by having a new outlet installed, or a closet door removed.

   - Figure out a new spot for whatever isn't working.

   You can see an example layout in Figure 11-1.

3. **Draw in the equipment you listed when performing Step 2 in the previous section.**

   Remember to indicate

   - Favorable directions

   - Placement of windows and doors

   - Location of electrical outlets and phone jacks

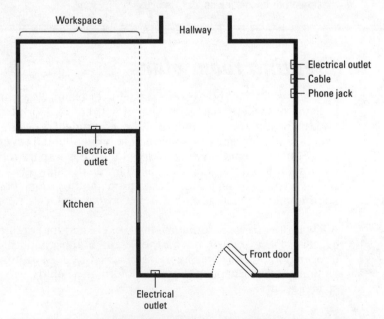

Figure 11-1: Don't forget to label all the outlets and jacks. You can see how the workspace has been marked off.

Outlets + Jacks = Cash

It can cost quite a bit of money to have electrical outlets and phone jacks installed, so pay particular attention to these elements as you're laying out your space. If you connect your computer modem to the phone jack that's already installed, you save yourself time and money. And don't forget that tangles of cords (such as extension cords) on the floor are dangerous and create negative chi.

You can cut little shapes from paper for ease of use and move them around the layout until you find a workable plan.

Just because you keep three-year-old tax returns under your desk now doesn't mean they have to stay there forever. Clutter is the enemy of Feng Shui. Be vigilant about keeping your workspace ready to roll. If you need help reducing clutter see Chapter 2.

Investing in Yourself: Swanky Equipment and Furnishings

All too often, people setting up home offices furnish them with cast-offs that formerly took up residence in the garage, the attic, the alley, or the basement. They use a folding table as a desk and an old paint-spattered kitchen chair to sit on. When people who furnish they're office with junk find they're not as productive in their home office as they thought they'd be, they wonder why!

Feng Shui says that our furnishings should be pleasing to us and should create a comfortable environment; they should also allow us to do our work with the minimum amount of hassle. Feng Shui emphasizes this key: Carefully select furniture and equipment that helps you do your job. This investment in your future will pay off countless times.

If you really love that ratty old desk because you wrote your first love letter at it, it's okay to hang onto it. Just because something is old doesn't mean it has to go on the trash heap. But if it makes your work difficult to do, maybe it should go in the playroom instead of your office.

Treat yourself to a home office that creates favorable energy. Toss that battered old filing cabinet that sticks every time you try to open a drawer, throw caution to the wind, and buy a new file cabinet. After tossing and before buying, keep in mind that these purchases are vital:

- ✔ **Desk.** See Chapter 8 for information on choosing a good desk for your workspace.

- ✔ **Desk chair.** See Chapter 8 for information on choosing the right desk chair for you.

- ✔ **Electronic equipment.** See Chapter 6 for information on arranging and dealing with electronic equipment.

- ✔ **Storage systems.** See Chapter 2 for more information on storage solutions.

Because electronic equipment can amount to some major debt, both financial and Feng Shui, keep this stuff in mind:

- ✔ **Try to keep your home office equipment to a minimum.** Purchase only equipment you *need* — in other words, get it only if it costs you money to do without it. For example, if you infrequently send or receive faxes, you can just go down to the copy center to fax. Chapter 6 discusses equipment and problems that you may encounter when using it. Just because you can buy a gadget and write it off as a deduction on your income taxes doesn't mean you need to.

- ✔ **Consider a multifunction machine.** If you need a scanner, a printer, and a copier, get one machine that does it all. Not only does this save space, but it also reduces the amount of equipment surrounding you.

- ✔ **Use services instead of equipment.** Voice mail service lets you get rid of that bulky answering machine, plus you can access it anywhere, anytime.

Nice and homey

Because you have freedom of choice in furnishing your home office, you can choose furnishings that appeal to you and have meaning to you. Jennifer uses a lovely old dresser to store supplies instead of an ugly office cabinet. You can store records in the trunk your grandmother passed on to you, or use the funky side table you found at the flea market to hold your inbox. These touches make your work environment even more pleasing and friendly.

Ensuring Success While Wearing Your Robe

Sometimes, your ability to Feng Shui your workspace is limited by what your company rules allow. Having a home office allows you free rein in creating a Feng Shui environment: Take advantage of it!

Use all the techniques you can to increase your prosperity and improve your chances of career success. Because your boss won't be stopping by your cubicle every half hour, you can go ahead and perform the Orange Peel Blessing explained in Chapter 15 without wondering what your co-workers think, hang all the wind chimes you want from the doorway, and create a collage of crystals on every available surface.

However, don't forget to keep the Feng Shui cures and elements in balance. Balancing the principles of Feng Shui in your home work-space can help you create the kind of welcoming, calm workspace that makes working from home a joy. See Figure 11-2 for an example of a well-designed home office.

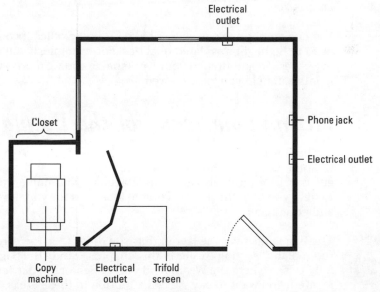

Figure 11-2: A well-designed home office.

Saying yes-yes to yin-yang

Most workspaces have more yang energy than yin energy because people bustle around doing their work, equipment hums, messengers make deliveries, and co-workers yak on the phone. But home workspaces tend to be more yin in character, particularly if you work alone, because much less action is happening there.

You may want things to be quiet and calm so you can get your work done, but if things are *too* quiet and calm, you find yourself snoozing instead of tracking down clients. In other words, workspaces should be slightly more yang than yin, and that's true of your home workspace, too. So when you're choosing the color to paint on your walls, find something a little more yang than you may otherwise consider selecting. See Chapter 5 for more information on choosing colors.

High-fiving the Five Elements

In Chapter 1 we describe the Five Elements and how keeping them balanced in your workspace can help keep *you* balanced in your workspace. You have free rein in your home workspace, but balance is key!

You can emphasize one element in your home office if you feel the need to highlight its related qualities. For example, if you're feeling overstressed and tired in your workspace, adding more water elements can help you feel renewed.

Fitting your room for the Bagua

In Chapter 1, we describe what the Bagua is and how to apply it. In Chapter 8, we show how to apply the Bagua to your desk. You've guessed it! You can also apply the Bagua to your home workspace to help you plan the most favorable locations for your furniture and equipment.

The Bagua fits over the layout that you drew. (See the "Creating room plans" section earlier in this chapter.) Study the Bagua carefully to see where the Wealth and Career Sectors in particular are located. You want to pay special attention to these areas, and may want to raise the chi by adding cures such as mirrors or water elements. (We can't overstress the importance of keeping your wastebasket out of that Wealth Sector!)

Chapter 12

Nestling into Nontraditional Workspaces

• •

In This Chapter

▶ Beginning to Feng Shui in strange surroundings

▶ Creating portable Feng Shui

• •

*N*ot everyone sits at a desk in a cubicle crunching numbers for the neighborhood insurance company. Many people don't work regular 9-to-5 jobs. More and more individuals are working as temps or as independent contractors and they often work in spaces that bear no resemblance to the traditional office — or even the traditional cube.

In this chapter we show you how to use Feng Shui in non-traditional workspaces. Whether you toil behind the counter at a clothing store or on the line at a factory; whether you design clown noses or study the mating habits of cockroaches, you can use some of the principles of Feng Shui to make your workspace more harmonious and inviting.

We cover strategies for workers in a wide variety of workspaces and offer suggestions for making Feng Shui portable — you *can* take it with you!

Working Outside the Cube

Many people, especially those in retail or service industries, have to share their workspaces. You may work the 8 a.m. to 4 p.m. shift at the cash register at the corner convenience mart, and someone else comes in and takes over your space at the end of your shift. Your mirror cure on the counter may make your co-workers nervous.

Desk sharing is also quite common. Call centers use this approach routinely — the first shift worker uses the same desk that the second shift worker uses. So neither worker really has a desk to call home.

When you have to share your workspace with other people, your Feng Shui efforts must be done with diplomacy and delicacy — but you can still Feng Shui your workspace. See Chapter 3 for more information about respecting other people's rights and needs while performing Feng Shui.

You want fries with that? Working behind the counter

You've got the mustard yellow uniform and the snazzy polyester hat. You've got the cash register in front of you and the warming table behind you. And you're saying, Feng Shui that?

You knew we wouldn't set up a scenario and then say, "Oops, sorry, we don't have any answers for you." Of course we have answers, and the answers aren't "quit your job" and "get a new one." Instead, remember the basic Feng Shui principles and use your imagination to help you apply them to your particular space. Figure 12-1 shows a great example of a service establishment with good Feng Shui; this architectural firm has a great space with great energy. The desks are arranged favorably; staggered and non-confrontational (not facing each other). They are also designed for the specific work being done. The short white wall on the left divides the space by function. Natural lighting is beneficial and good Feng Shui. Pathways are clear and people can move around easily. The finishing touches will come when plants and natural fiber carpeting are added to balance the brick and metal.

You'll need to check with your boss for the rules, and if he puts the kibosh on hanging crystals from the rafters, try something a little subtler. Do what you can and remember that it's your intentions that count.

Try this:

> ✔ **Clear the clutter!** Keep the area around your register clean and neat, at least while you're working your shift.

✔ **Add a few personal elements to your workspace while you're working.** For example, if you run one of seven cash registers at the grocery store, bring a portable Bagua.

✔ **Wear your Feng Shui.** A nice crystal bracelet can raise the chi in your work environment, and who could object? For more on this turn to Chapter 15.

Figure 12-1: Feng Shui concepts at work.

Trucking in your four-wheeled office

Lots of service and sales people, among others, spend most of their waking moments in their cars getting from Point A to Point B. For people who transport goods for a living, their vehicles are their offices.

Hanging ornaments from the rearview mirror is discouraged, as they can interfere with your field of vision and distract you as you drive. Leaving loose objects around is also discouraged, as these can go flying through the air if you have to brake quickly. That Bagua mirror isn't going to do you any good if it shatters!

So how do you Feng Shui your car? Take a look at the following guidelines:

- ✔ **Choose a vehicle color that is more yin.** This helps balance the yang energy that being in a moving vehicle creates. Red cars have very powerful yang energy. Blue or black are good choices.

- ✔ **Keep your automobile clean and free of clutter.** The windows should be kept clean and free of dust and grease. Clean those fries out from under your seat, too!

- ✔ **Maintain good working order.** Rattles and squeaks should be attended to so that you don't feel stressed by them.

- ✔ **Use aromatherapy oils.** Rosemary and lemon are especially good for helping drivers remain calm and attentive. You can put a handful of potpourri in the ashtray to give your vehicle a pleasant scent.

Often, service workers do their work on other people's property. If you're a plumber, for instance, you go to people's houses and fix their plumbing. Because you're constantly in and out of people's homes and businesses, it's challenging to Feng Shui your work-space. Kinda hard to hang a crystal cure under Mr. Brown's kitchen sink while he's waiting for you to unclog the pipes. In addition to using Feng Shui in your car, see this chapter's "Packing a Portable Feng Shui Kit" to find other Feng Shui options for road warriors.

Donning your hard hat: Factories and warehouses

Helloooooo in there . . . Factories and warehouses seem like the last place Feng Shui is possible — all that vast echoing space, all those conveyor belts, all that lack of personal space. But remember, Feng Shui is more than hanging crystals and positioning mirrors. If you can't always use the visible components of Feng Shui, use the invisible components: Use your intentions! See Chapter 1 for more about intentions. In other words, if you're working on a factory line and you can't add a nice green plant to your part of the conveyor belt, all is not lost.

Feng Shui what you can. If you can't Feng Shui your part of the con-veyor belt, then Feng Shui your lunchbox! Feng Shui your locker or even Feng Shui your break room. (See Chapter 13 for more informa-tion.) Two key concepts of Feng Shui work anywhere:

✔ **Clear the clutter:** Almost any workspace benefits from this. Even if it isn't your job to sweep the floor, you can take the initiative and clean up to make a more harmonious workspace.

✔ **Set your intentions:** If you want to reduce the stress you feel when working with your co-workers, but can't do anything to enhance the chi, try this: As you arrive for work in the morning, set your intentions. Tell yourself, "I am going to work hard to get along with my co-workers, because it will make my work life more enjoyable and it may result in bonuses all around." You may be amazed at the difference this can make.

Turn to Chapter 9 for more information on using Feng Shui in Open Concept offices. Many of the same ideas apply to factories and similar workspaces.

They aren't a Motown band: Temps and contractors

If you're only going to be working somewhere for a few weeks until someone returns from maternity leave, it may not seem worth the effort to Feng Shui your workspace. But it is. Short-term employees and independent contractors often feel unconnected to their working environment, never really settling in. And feeling unconnected interferes with productivity, makes you restless, and can result in irritability and frustration when dealing with other (especially permanent) employees. That's no way to live, even if only for three weeks!

By applying some of the principles of Feng Shui to your workspace, you take ownership of that space. You feel more welcomed and calm when you're at work; an especially important consideration if any co-workers resent your presence or ignore you.

A couple of cures in the right place (think Career sector, Helpful People, and Wealth sector) and that temporary job may turn into a full-time position!

Before you Feng Shui anything as a temp get permission! You may be working in someone else's workspace, and they might not appreciate the lovely robin's egg blue you painted the walls.

Of course you don't have a lot of choice when you're a temp. Someone says, "Sit there," and you do it. If you balk, the boss may just call the temp agency and ask for someone new. But you can do a few things to feel more in control of your environment. These fixes can help:

✔ **Clear the clutter!** Allow the chi to flow easily through any workspace. Trust us, no one minds if you empty all the trash-cans and pick up all the Diet Coke cans.

✔ **Place yourself in a power position.** See Chapter 14 for more information on power positions.

- **Face your most auspicious direction (see Chapter 1 to find out what this is). Sit with your back to a wall.**

- **Sit so that you have the widest view of the room in front of you.**

- **Sit so you can see the doorway.** Temps often need to make quick escapes.

✔ **Avoid sitting where cutting chi from sharp angles can flow directly toward you.** Cutting comments from co-workers can be sharp enough for the temp. (See Chapter 2 for more information on cutting chi.)

✔ **Apply principles where you can.** For example, if you're a salesperson with a desk at headquarters, Feng Shui your desk.

✔ **Set your intentions.** As you add a cure, think about and then say to yourself *why* you're doing it. "By placing a crystal cure in the Career sector, I am reinforcing my goal of finding a permanent position with one of the employers for whom I am now a temporary employee."

✔ **Place a portable Bagua on your desk or work surface.** This helps you apply the principles of Feng Shui and to reinforce your intentions. Chapter 3 tells you more about the Bagua.

✔ **Bring an object that makes you feel good and keep it where you can see it.** Possibilities are a framed picture of someone you love, a beautiful card, or an attractive ornament.

Packing a Portable Feng Shui Kit

If your job takes you to different locations or you can't leave your Feng Shui design elements permanently in place, create a portable *Feng Shui kit,* a collection of items you keep together and take with you. See Figure 12-2 for an example of a Feng Shui kit.

Figure 12-2: Feng Shui on the go.

Feng Shui on the move. Create a kit that you can bring with you and place on your desktop or tabletop or even the floor by your feet if you have no other choice. (If you're really limited, you can wear your Feng Shui; see Chapter 15.)

Here's how to put together that portable Feng Shui kit:

1. **Select your Feng Shui items.**

   • **Keep your objects small and simple.** Portability is key. Your piano is probably not a good choice.

   • **Throw in your beloveds.** As you're selecting objects that represent the various elements or a sector on the Bagua, try to find things that are personally meaning-ful to you and that you enjoy looking at — in other words, objects that make your heart smile.

   • **Smell good on the road.** Aromatherapy lifts your spirits and energizes you. Carry a spritzer bottle of your favorite fragrance or aromatic oil and spritz just before you start work or when you feel stressed. Chapter 15 has more aromatherapy details.

- **Choose objects that symbolize each of the Five Elements and all nine Life Sectors.** The nine Life Sectors are associated with the Five Elements, so choose objects that can represent one of the Five Elements and a Life Sector at the same time.

2. **Place all items in one location.**

3. **Include something on which to set your objects.**

   Use a small Bagua-shaped mirror or cut a piece of felt or other fabric into the Bagua's octagonal shape.

4. **Wrap the objects in a silk scarf or a piece of velvet.**

   The idea is to protect the contents; they can be wrapped in anything. Silk and velvet are beautiful and do the job perfectly. Use whatever works for you.

TIP

Holly's Portable Feng Shui Kit

Holly's kit contains a small Bagua-shaped mirror on which to place the objects. She bought the mirror at an Asian gift store for $3.00, so your investment in a portable Feng Shui kit does not have to be high!

Here's what she uses for objects to represent the Nine Life Sectors and the Five Elements:

✔ Career: Very small abalone shell. The shell symbolizes the Water element.

✔ Wealth: A lucky Chinese coin in a traditional red envelope.

✔ Children/Creativity: Picture of her children in a small metal frame.

✔ Knowledge and Spirituality: Small ceramic angel. The ceramic material symbolizes the Earth element.

✔ Fame: Pyramid-shaped crystal on red felt. The pyramid shape symbolizes the Fire element.

✔ Helpful People: Tiny gold charm with beads representing friends and clients. The metal charm symbolizes the Metal element.

✔ Family: Small wooden carved blue bird that reminds her of her parents. The wood and the blue symbolize the Wood element.

✔ Relationships: A rock (Earth element) with the word *Love* stamped on it.

✔ Tai Chi/Health: A small yin-yang medallion.

Take a look at Figure 12-2 for a closer look at Holly's kit.

5. **Place the scarf or velvet in a pouch or box.**

   The pouch or box can be tucked into your purse, backpack, or briefcase and taken to any location.

6. **Set your intention as you create and use your portable Feng Shui kit.**

   Setting an intention can be something like, "As I place these special objects in my work place, I want to bring harmony to myself and my co-workers and raise the chi in this space to achieve the best work possible." This can be said aloud or just inside your head.

Chapter 13

Breaking Into Rooms: Waiting, Storage, and Bath

. . . .

In This Chapter

▶ Deciding on strategy

▶ Sitting down to think about waiting rooms

▶ Making the most out of the mailroom

▶ Giving yourself a great meeting room

▶ Creating a restful restroom

. . . .

The copy room, the employee break room, the waiting room, the storage room, the bathroom: These communal areas get a lot of use but not a lot of attention — except from us. By applying the principles of Feng Shui to these spaces, you can make employees feel more appreciated and you may even increase productivity.

We also describe how important it is to locate these rooms in the right place — putting the bathroom right next to the CEO's office can flush profits right down the drain! But never fear we have cures for unfavorable placements, too.

 Even if you're not in charge of the copy room, you can take the initiative and encourage your boss and co-workers to apply some Feng Shui principles to these neglected areas. Don't forget, some of the basic keys to Feng Shui are also fairly easy to get others to agree to — like keeping an area clutter-free and organized. But it all depends on you taking the lead and making it happen!

In this chapter we show you how to Feng Shui this space. Keep in mind that how you balance the Five Elements (and other principles) in various rooms depends on how each room is used. Function comes first.

Making a Plan and Working It

If you're not the boss, you probably need the boss' approval to make Feng Shui changes to waiting areas, storage rooms, and other communal areas.

Develop a step-by-step plan for convincing the head cheese (and co-workers) to apply Feng Shui to shared areas:

1. **Decide what area(s) could benefit most from applying a few simple Feng Shui principles.**

   The disorganized mess that is the copy room is a good prospect.

2. **Develop a checklist of ways to combat the problems these rooms present.**

   Focus on devising simple Feng Shui solutions like clearing the clutter, storing items out of sight, and providing easy access to often-used items. At this early stage, you don't need to talk about the Five Elements and yin versus yang energy, especially if you're not sure how your boss and co-workers will respond to that.

3. **Approach the head honcho with your ideas.**

   Offer to do the work during your time off (but save this as a negotiating tool. You may be able to get the boss to pay you to Feng Shui!).

4. **Explain that a clutterless copy room increases productivity and decreases frustration.**

5. **Yay! You got the go-ahead.**

6. **Start with one small project.**

   Try clearing out a closet or reorganizing a storage space.

7. **Report to the boss when that project is complete.**

   Share any positive feedback you've received. Back up your report with hard stats (assuming you can get some). Once you've assured the boss of the bottom-line benefit of Feng Shui, bring up another step you want to take. Before you know it, it's possible that everyone in the entire building will be eager to Feng Shui!

If you are the boss, you can follow the same plan to convince employees to go along with the changes you want to make.

Have a Seat: Reception Areas

Many managers and owners don't spend much time in their own waiting rooms or reception areas. They may not realize how important it is to present a welcoming image by designing and maintaining these rooms appropriately.

In fact, they may never really "see" these rooms — especially the way a first-time client or customer might. So, if you're the boss, take a look at these areas as if you're seeing them for the first time. If you're not the boss, then use your own eyes and relay what you see to the person in charge.

Because the waiting room or reception area tells a visitor a great deal about your business, it's important to deliberately and constructively decide what message you want to send. If you want people to feel that you're a solid, well established, dependable corporation, you might furnish the reception area with antiques and paneled walls, which are more yin in character. If you want to convince clients that you're a chic, hip, and innovative company, you might go for a more yang presentation with glossy walls, more metal, and vivid or contrasting colors.

Regardless of the message you want to communicate to others, you need to keep the principles of Feng Shui in balance. Too much yin energy leaves your visitors snoozing in the waiting room and too much yang energy has them running out the door. Turn to Chapters 1 and 3 for more information on putting the principles of Feng Shui into action.

See Figure 13-1 for an example of a well-designed and well-maintained entry area.

Getting an impression of a client's first impression

When clients, employees, investors, and delivery people walk in your front door, the waiting room or reception area is usually the first thing they see. (In Jennifer's house the first thing they see is a large fluffy Alaskan malamute, but that's a different story.)

Plants would help balance the brick.

Natural light raises chi.

This curving wall helps move chi through the space.

The natural-fiber carpeting being added will warm the space.

Figure 13-1: This is one well-designed entry area.

You want clients and others to get a good impression as soon as they walk in the door. If they think you don't care about your building, they may think you don't care about your products or services. So you need to see these areas the way a visitor might, and you need to look at them with Feng Shui eyes:

Walk in your front door and note what you see, hear, and smell.

> ✔ **Are the sights, sounds and smells appealing?** If they're appealing to you, do you think they appeal to most people? You may love the smell of fresh gasoline, for instance, but your customers very well may not.

> ✔ **Do you feel welcome? Comfortable?** Listen to your intuition.

> ✔ **Is the area neat and clean?**

✔ **Can you easily tell where to go to find Accounting or PR?** Signage should be clear and easy to understand.

✔ **Do angles, edges, and energetic arrows create cutting chi?** Chapter 2 has more on chi.

✔ **Does the furniture arrangement allow chi to freely flow?**

✔ **What elements are out of proportion?** Be aware that overhead beams can make workers and visitors feel subtly threatened.

If you feel welcome and at ease in the entry area, that's a good start. If you don't feel welcome, make a checklist of the reasons why: dirt tracked on the floor, a huge skull and crossbones flag, or just really ugly carpeting. Then, using your Feng Shui eyes (and your Feng Shui knowledge), look more deeply into the area and see what else might be causing the negative energy. Are the colors subtly wrong? Do sharp corners send cutting chi toward you? Is your receptionist extremely sarcastic?

Keeping clutter from clients

Yes, we know we've told you a thousand times, but we're telling you again: clutter is the enemy of Feng Shui. Not only is it unattractive, but it also interferes with the free movement of chi.

The reception and waiting areas should be kept clean and neat at all times. These ideas can help:

✔ **If the building has double doors, both should be operable and in use.** Otherwise, chi can get stuck and may create negative energy.

✔ **Invest in cabinets instead of open file shelves.** Not only does this look more attractive, but it can also prevent cutting chi from creating negative energy in the area.

✔ **Keep the reception desk uncluttered and welcoming.** If the receptionist has additional work to do besides greeting clients, the work should be something that can easily be put aside and doesn't create an unsightly mess.

✔ **If you provide reading materials for visitors, make sure the material is in good condition and looks attractive.** Replace dog-eared magazines and put out fresh brochures when the old ones look tired.

- If you offer beverages to clients, make certain spills are quickly cleaned up and that used paper products and dirty dishes are quickly whisked out of sight.

- **Keep the wastebasket accessible but unobtrusive.** People often have trash on hand when they walk into a building; give them a place to put it other than on the floor! Consider a wastebasket with a lid so that no one has to look at the trash inside.

- **Add plants and water features.** This helps things look fresh and increases positive, natural chi.

Pulling up a chair

Furnishings for reception areas and waiting rooms should be comfortable and attractive. Take the color and texture of upholstery into consideration as you choose. Chapter 5 has detailed information on color and texture. For a quick overview, see Table 13-1.

Follow these furniture-shopping rules:

- **Choose for function and design.** If you're choosing chairs for a doctor's waiting room and people may have to sit on the chairs for a half an hour at a time, the chairs should be comfortable.

Soothing the senses with water

Aquariums in the reception area help set the right tone for your business. The movement of the fish is calming and relaxing. Aquariums are a Water element and can seem nurturing and supportive to visitors.

- Make certain the aquarium is in proportion to the room.

- It should be large enough for the fish to swim easily.

- Stock it with natural materials instead of plastic plants and artificial seaweed.

- Don't let the water get murky, keep the aquarium glass clean, and when a fish goes belly-up, dispose of it immediately. Otherwise, you create a bad impression and may negatively affect chi.

Traditionally, Feng Shui aquariums are stocked with nine (a lucky number) fish, eight gold and one black. The black one symbolically attracts negative energy so that it doesn't go elsewhere in the building.

Testing for comfort

Always test furniture first before buying it and placing it. If you can, have people of different sizes and ages test the furniture. The soft comfy armchair that you enjoy sinking into may be difficult for an older person to struggle out of; the sofa that's just right for you may be uncomfortable for someone who is shorter or taller.

✔ **Select furnishings with rounded corners.** This helps prevent sending out energetically negative chi. It helps increase the flow of the beneficial chi through the space, which may subtly communicate to visitors that they'll find a lot of good energy in the office and that their needs will be seen to quickly.

✔ **Place the furniture so that chi can flow smoothly. Furniture shouldn't be arranged in rows that block the chi, or grouped tightly together giving the chi nowhere to go.**

✔ **Pick natural materials for your furnishings.** Natural is good Feng Shui! Remember that Feng Shui had its origin in honoring and respecting Mother Nature. Four thousand years later this ancient common sense is still working: Think natural!

 In reception areas, it's okay for the chi to move more quickly than in other parts of the office, as long as people don't have to wait long in the reception room. If chi flows fairly quickly, you get the sensation that this is a place where work gets done, and that may be exactly the right impression you want visitors to have. However, in waiting rooms where people have to wait for extended periods of time, it may be better to arrange the furniture to slow the chi down, so that people feel more relaxed and not as hurried.

Waiting on the Five Elements

How you balance the elements in a waiting room depends on how you want your clients to feel when you greet and work with them. Table 13-1 gives the breakdown.

✔ **Chill out.** If you want people to relax as they're waiting (maybe especially important for a dentist!), include the yin aspect of the various elements. If you're going to use green in the room, make it a dark forest green for its soothing properties. Emphasizing the Earth element in waiting rooms can help visitors feel centered and grounded, a good thing if they're about to get a root canal! A fountain would be an ideal addition here with its tranquil and pleasing sound.

✔ **Rev up.** Maybe you're trying to sell your super-fast-speedy-print process. If you want visitors to feel more energized, emphasize the yang aspect of the elements. Choose a striking red accent color on the walls, for example, or emphasize the Fire Element because that's associated with decisive action.

Table 13-1 Textures and Colors and Their Yin and Yang

More Yin	More Yang
Highly textured items	Smooth, highly polished items
Dark colors (like black and navy blue)	Bright colors (like yellow and red)

Making a Chi Break for Copy, Mail, and Storage Rooms

Mailrooms, copy rooms, storage rooms, break rooms and such make up some of the most neglected areas in office buildings — even though people spend a lot of time in these areas. If your storage room is tremendously cluttered you use up good energy and create stress and tension every time you have to spend 20 minutes hunting down a new box of paperclips. When you go into the break room for a breather and all you're greeted with are plastic chairs and faux-wood table tops sticky with spilled pop, you're not getting much of a break.

Each of these kinds of rooms faces different Feng Shui problems. Take a look at Table 13-2 for pointers on tackling those problems.

Taking a bite out of attrition

Studies show that having negative feelings about your work and your working environment leads to high turnover rates. So create positive chi in your work environment and you may retain employees longer!

Table 13-2		Rooms and Their Obstacles	
Room	*The room's function*	*Common problems*	*Solutions*
Work/copy room	Filing, faxing, printing. Can be yang energy.	Tend to have an abundance of the Metal element, such as filing cabinets and tables for spreading out files.	• Fire elements such as non-glare lighting or spark-ling windows. Artwork with red adds enthusiasm. • Lush plants — on top of filing cabinets or in a dreary corner — would go a long way to help get the work done!
Break room	Serves a restful function allowing employees a place to escape the yang activity in the main office and relax.	Clutter abounds: magazines stacked, coffee cups left around. Sometimes serves as a storage room for objects with no other home. Tend to be bare and utilitarian.	• Place yin, soothing colors, round tables and comfortably upholstered seating. • Clutter needs to be kept to a minimum: coffee cups kept in closed cupboards and reading material in a basket instead of on top of the tables. • Plants encourage relaxation and this area would greatly benefit from a fountain.

(continued)

Table 13-2 *(continued)*

Room	The room's function	Common problems	Solutions
Mail room	Ship and distribute letters and packages to people inside and outside of the building. Depending on the amount of activity tends toward yang energy.	Lots of metal makes for lack of balance. Clutter is a problem. Cutting chi from sharp edges (everything from mailboxes to letters) may create a tense environment.	• Wood and Fire elements can help balance the Metal element. • Adding plants and other living objects can improve beneficial chi. (Take your dog to work day, anyone?) • Shelving and other work surfaces with rounded edges can reduce cutting chi.
Storage room	Space for keeping supplies and equipment not used regularly. Usually a yin environment.	Clutter blocking chi.	• Mirrors can help create the illusion of space. • Storage spaces need good lighting to illuminate all the stuff. A faceted crystal can't hurt. • Use of plants would be great, even silk ones are better than leaving this space bereft of the wood element.

Copy rooms, storage rooms, and mailrooms often become the places to stash everything that doesn't have another home. Pretty soon the piles of old appliances, discarded pantomime horse outfits, and outdated files overwhelm the space. Chi needs to flow freely throughout a space. It shouldn't move too quickly, but it also shouldn't stagnate and collect in the corners where all the old computer equipment is stored.

Clearing a path from the fax to the printer

Your main priority is to clear pathways and traffic areas in and around the room. People need to move into and out of the room without scraping their shins on anything. If you have to move three boxes and an old metal desk to get to the coffee maker supplies, it's time to clear some pathways.

Mentally map out pathways and keep them clear. Or literally map out the traffic areas and pathways to make certain that equipment and supplies are readily accessible once you've reorganized everything.

1. **Draw a room layout (as shown in Chapter 3).**

2. **Identify structural features.**

   This includes windows, doors, columns, and posts. For this layout, also draw in electrical outlets, wall switches, and furniture placement to make certain that all items in use are easy to get to.

Getting some breathing room

All of these rooms need to be well ventilated so chi flows smoothly and unpleasant odors and fumes dissipate. In particular, areas where electronic equipment and supplies are kept should have good ventilation that allows fresh air to circulate, to prevent the toxic materials and harsh chemicals found in toners and other supplies from adversely affecting workers.

Windows that actually open are one of the best sources of ventilation and fresh air, but they're hard to find in modern buildings. If you can't open the windows, use fans, keep doors open, keep heat registers dust-free, and make certain that the ductwork in the room is clean. See Chapter 6 for more information on the problems electronic equipment can cause, and Chapter 7 for more information about medical problems caused by office building environments and the materials commonly found in office buildings.

3. **Using arrows show how traffic flows into, out of, and around the room.**

4. **Allow at least 36 inches of width for traffic aisles.**

5. **Put back only those things that are necessary for the room to fulfill its function.**

   In other words, the break room shouldn't also double as the storage room because the storage room is too full. Do you have typewriter ribbons on hand? Pitch them! Or at least store them somewhere else.

   - Get rid of broken equipment, outdated electronics, and unneeded files.

   - Find offsite storage for old records that need to be kept somewhere but which are not accessed regularly.

   - Put an ad in the paper to sell furnishings and equipment that you no longer need. Then use the profits to buy pizza for everyone involved in the cleaning up process!

   - Don't be afraid to throw things away. Recycle if you can, of course, but get rid of the dead wood! (No, we don't mean the guy in the next cubicle.)

6. **Ensure that all work areas have appropriate lighting.**

   Evaluate the workstations for the type of lighting that is most helpful. Indirect lighting may be fine over the copy machine, because fine detail work is not done there, but more powerful direct lighting may be needed elsewhere. See Chapter 4 for more information about lighting workspaces.

7. **Choose the most effective ways to store your things.**

   - Select closed cabinets when possible.

   - Use file drawers and cabinets rather than open shelves.

   - Use clear boxes to store piles of miscellaneous items and mark on the outside of each box what it contains.

Putting some pillows on that printer

Mail, copy, and storage rooms often consist primarily of metal furniture with sharp angles. These angles and corners can create *sha* chi; cutting, negative chi that makes people feel uncomfortable, unwelcome, and which energetically depresses the level of good chi in the whole office. More on chi in Chapter 2.

Try these cures:

✔ Replace some metal cabinets with containers with rounded corners.

✔ Add plants to camouflage problem areas.

✔ Use round baskets for storage.

✔ Drape material over open shelves to hide the mess from view.

Keeping the space sparse

Once you've de-cluttered and reorganized the utilitarian rooms, keep these spaces clean and orderly. Keeping up with this basic maintenance extends the life of the spaces and contributes to more positive chi throughout the entire building.

✔ **Make the process part of everyone's job.** In other words, if you spill, you clean it up. Put a sign up, enlist your boss's help, rotate KP duty among all staffers, or pool your lunch money and hire someone.

✔ **Frequently paint or thoroughly clean the walls to make them seem fresh and appealing.**

✔ **Professionally maintain equipment so that it remains in good working order.** Instead of waiting for the copy machine to break down before paying anyone to service it, invest in routine servicing and maintenance.

✔ **At least once a year, inspect these rooms and have any problems repaired.** Wobbly storage shelves need to be fixed. Uneven tables should be leveled. Replace broken tiles.

See Figure 13-2 for an example of a well-designed break room.

Cupboards keep messy, unattractive objects under wraps.

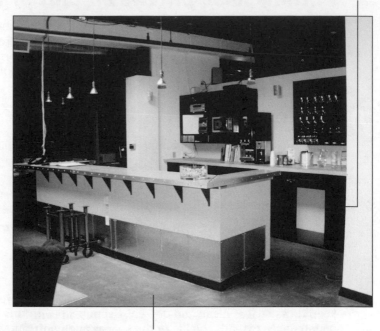

Stools upholstered in natural materials will help balance the metal.

Figure 13-2: Add a couple of plants, and this break area is on its way to being Feng Shui!

Ergonomics in the copy room

Equipment must be easily accessible in your copy room, and cords and cables need to be carefully secured and tucked away so that they don't trip anyone up. Any hazardous materials must be clearly labeled and treated as toxic.

If people spend much time folding, collating, or mailing materials, provide a table with good chairs so that workers don't spend hours on their feet twisting and reaching in ergonomically unsound ways.

Post instructions for using the equipment correctly in the area. A designated person can be in charge of the equipment so that everyone knows whom to contact when the copier jams, rather than skinning their knuckles trying to fix something they don't know how to fix. Keep Information on servicing readily available so that equipment problems and failures don't unduly disrupt the work environment. In Chapter 8, we discuss ergonomics in more detail.

Calling a Meeting: Conference and Board Rooms

Meeting rooms are generally designed for function. Although some organizations make an effort to create attractive meeting rooms, designers often rely on neutral tones for the walls and furniture. This is a good approach in moderation, but the entire area can seem unappealing and boring if everything is neutral. Neutral and boring does not create positive chi. In fact, it's common for conference rooms to be so yin as to make everyone fall asleep when they should be making important decisions.

Don't be afraid to be bold with color and texture once in a while! One wall done in a rich tone (such as hunter green, burgundy, or Tuscan gold) can spark up an entire room. A rich-looking tapestry hung on a prominent wall can bring the whole space to life. Artwork in bright colors makes the space more attractive and turns a yin space into a yang space.

See Figure 13-3 for an example of a well-designed conference room. The framed photos of favorite places are a good Feng Shui touch. The windows provide natural light and the leather chairs are comfortable and nicely rounded. The two statues on the table were chosen for sentimental reason and the room has plenty of free space so that visitors can move freely. It might be a good touch to move the plant that's visible through the doorway into the room to raise chi.

Meeting with the Five Elements

Often, meeting rooms consist of a large space with a conference table and chairs, perhaps some equipment for making presentations, with little room for other furnishings. But you can still have all Five Elements present if you use your creativity. See Chapters 1 and 3 for more information on the Five Elements.

When you only have room for a table, use color and texture to balance the elements. Don't forget that yang colors include red, orange, and yellow and yin colors include purple, green, blue and black.

Figure 13-3: You can brainstorm till the cows come home in this well-designed conference room.

Here are some tips for livening up a meeting room, so that meetings reach their conclusions faster (instead of being time-wasters) and people stay awake during the lecture on Hazardous Materials Management:

 ✔ **Paint the walls a more vibrant color if you want people to move more quickly.**

 ✔ **Choose interesting fabric for window coverings.**

 ✔ **Hang paintings that symbolize one or more of the elements.**

Feeling pretty powerful, eh?

The person at the head of a rectangular table is in a *power position:* a physical position that enhances the appearance of strength and confidence. (See Chapter 14 for more on using power positions to enhance career success.) When you sit at a conference table, always try to sit facing the doorway, but not directly looking out the doorway. Or face your most auspicious direction (see Chapter 1 to learn what this is). Try to sit so your back is supported with a wall; don't sit with your back to the door or a window. Using a larger chair (or one with a higher back) than the other people in the room gives the subtle impression of more power.

> ✔ **Add lively chi by placing plants or fresh flowers in an attractive vase in the center of the conference table.** Keep the arrangement low so that people can see over it.

A meeting of the minds on chairs

The right furnishings for a meeting room depend on what you're trying to accomplish there. See Table 13-3 for more information.

Table 13-3 Accomplishing What You Want with Design	
What you want	*How to get it*
To encourage quick brainstorming sessions	Choose round tables that encourage faster movement of chi.
To encourage more deliberative decision-making	Place a large, rectangular table in the room.
To ensure deliberate but shared decision making	A good compromise choice is an oval-shaped table, which still has a clear "head of the table" position, but is less rigid and solid than a rectangular table.
To avoid making your employees feel exposed and vulnerable	Avoid glass tables.

Treating the Water Closet with a Little Respect

Bathrooms are where water, which signifies abundance, drains away. Just imagine a toilet flushing your dollar bills away to get an idea of what the toilet signifies in Feng Shui. On the day-to-day level, bathrooms are designed for the elimination of waste, and so we connect them with dirtiness. Bathrooms also have drains — the sinks, the toilets — that can flush away energy in a building.

Metal and ceramic, which relate to Metal and Earth elements, are the main materials used in bathrooms. To balance them, add more Wood elements. Obviously you don't need a tabletop fountain in a space already filled to capacity with the Water element. Try plants and flowers, wood objects, and things in green and blue.

Putting the potty in its place

If you cringe at the thought of flushing those afore-mentioned dollar bills down the toilet, you'll want to make sure your bathrooms are not in a position to bankrupt your business. Locate the loo away from

- **Places where important business is conducted:** Because the bathroom can give off unpleasant sights and odors, it can be an unattractive room.

- **The center of a space:** The center of the floor plan represents the T'ai Chi or overall well-being of the energetic space . . . this can drain the health and energy of the business away.

- **Workspaces:** The room can create negative energy or drain good energy from a space.

- **The front entrance:** The chi entering the building goes right out and down the drains. And when you enter a building, the lavatory shouldn't be one of the first rooms you see.

- **The Wealth sector:** This can lead to the flushing away of profits.

- **Being easily visible when the door is open:** Keep the bathroom door closed at all times, and gentlemen, if the toilet has a lid, please put it down after use!

But a business without bathrooms isn't going to work very well. So where *can* you put the toilets? Toward the back of the building, away from workspaces.

Another way to create positive chi in the lavatory is using natural materials: Put potpourri in wicker baskets and use unglazed brick or terracotta tiles on the floor. Place plants in ceramic containers. Avoiding unnecessary harsh chemicals is another boon to the bath. Abrasive, dangerous chemicals are the opposite of Feng Shui principles, which encourage the use of natural materials whenever possible.

Check the chi in the bathroom

One of the ways to cut down on the negative associations people have with bathrooms is to keep the ones in your space scrupulously clean. This requires more than hiring a janitor — it also requires educating employees and others about cleaning up after themselves. If someone splashes water all over the floor, they either clean it themselves or alert the appropriate person that a bucket and mop are needed.

Check bathrooms that see a lot of use every hour. Those used less frequently should still be attended to once or twice a day. Wastebaskets need to be emptied, counters and mirrors wiped, messes on the floor attended to, toilet bowls cleansed, and supplies restocked.

Bathrooms can also be made more appealing by keeping them fresh smelling. Add baskets of potpourri to release a pleasant scent (as opposed to using chemical, unnatural air fresheners). A citrus orange scented air spray is probably one of the best to use; they are readily available at most grocery and drug stores. Place plants throughout the room to add more positive, living energy to the space. Artwork, ornaments, candles, and other decorative items help make the bathroom a more appealing space.

Working near the porcelain god

If you can hear the flush every time someone uses the toilet, that's not a good sign. Try to get your desk moved, or at least encourage the boss to put insulation around the place!

If that's not possible, try these cures:

- ✔ **Keep the bathroom door shut.**

- ✔ **If you can see the toilet from your workspace when the door is open, hang a crystal from the ceiling between the toilet and the door to help make the toilet symbolically invisible.**

- ✔ **Hang a mirror on the bathroom door.** This helps remind people to keep the bathroom door shut, and deflects chi away from the bathroom and back into the main part of the building where it can do some good.

- ✔ **If possible, keep toilet lids down at all times.** Many commercial bathrooms toilets are not equipped with lids.

Part IV
Interacting with Others: Implementing for Success

The 5th Wave
By Rich Tennant

"Well, right off I can tell the Feng Shui of your interrogation room is all off. The Life Area is in conflict with the Knowledge Area which creates a very powerful Alibi Area right over here."

In this part . . .

To get along in business, you have to play well with others. And Feng Shui can help you! This part describes how to use the principles of Feng Shui to enhance your career success, whether you're an entry-level employee, the CEO, or a footloose freelancer.

In this part, we also show how you can wear your Feng Shui so that no matter where you go and what you're doing, you feel powerful and confident.

Chapter 14

Personal Power and Successful Work Relationships

. . . .

In This Chapter

▶ Developing personal power

▶ Using Feng Shui to create strong interpersonal relationships

▶ Understanding the connection between relationships and wealth

. . . .

*T*his chapter shows you how to apply Feng Shui principles to enhance *personal power* — your own feelings of strength and confidence and how you project these feelings to others. Having personal power can translate into business success, as you will actually be more assured and effective in your job.

You can achieve personal power by designing your workspace to take advantage of certain power positions. *Power positions* are ways to physically place your body to affect how others perceive your strength and confidence. Deliberate intention setting helps reinforce this perception.

We also show how Feng Shui can help you create useful, harmonious relationships. By forging strong relationships with your boss, co-workers, and clients, you can enhance your career success and add more happiness and joy to your life.

Enhancing your power in the workplace increases the likelihood that you will become a more important part of the business and an important part of its power structure. That will almost certainly improve your career prospects. By feeling and appearing stronger and more confident, you can take on more challenging assignments and positions, again increasing your career success.

But obviously you can't have career success without other people. You have bosses and co-workers and clients who are essential to your career. Convincing them to perceive you as an effective, competent worker results in increased career success for you. If you can't get along with your clients, they'll go elsewhere. If your co-workers complain about your attitude, your boss will hesitate before placing you in a supervisory position.

Voting for Best Couple: Feng Shui and Relationships

In Feng Shui philosophy, relationships with other people are very influential. If you look at the Bagua, you can see that the Life Sectors influence your connections with other people: Traditional Chinese Feng Shui places North at the bottom and South at the top of the compass! The South sector, also called Fame, is related to how others perceive you. The Southwest sector is the Marriage sector (in your work environment, this might be better thought of as the Relationship sector); the West sector is the Children (and Creativity) sector; the Northwest sector is the Helpful People sector; and the East sector is the Family sector. The other sectors also have some connection to other people — for example, success in the Career sector (North) relies on your ability to communicate your value to other people. Obviously, other people are very important! Figure 14-1 shows a Bagua for your easy reference.

The Bagua's Life Sectors emphasize the importance of communicating and relating with others. Overall well being is the bottom-line goal of Feng Shui — you achieve overall well being by fostering strong personal relationships within your family, office, and the community at large.

The nature of chi also emphasizes the importance of relationships. *Chi,* life energy, flows throughout the universe. Each of us creates and responds to it; each of us can raise or lower it in a given space. So when my chi collides with your chi, the results can be beneficial or unfavorable to you, me, or both of us.

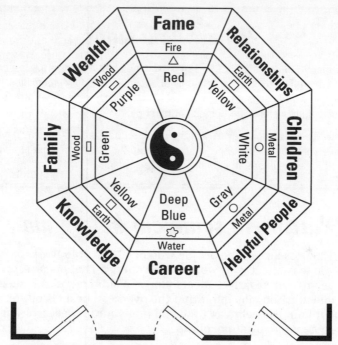

Figure 14-1: The Bagua shows the importance of relationships in all of the Life Sectors.

Your what is connected to my what?

The chi within us all is interconnected. You've probably had the experience where you were having a good day, but then your best friend called you in tears, and pretty soon you weren't having such a good day. You felt her energy affect yours, which is only natural.

Because everyone's chi is interconnected, you can affect other people's chi by creating positive energy. People are attracted to vibrant, happy, active individuals; they're not so attracted to glum, down-in-the-dumps souls who suck energy from everyone around them. So can you see how being vibrant, happy, and active is in your best interest? Chapter 1 tells you best how to get happy.

Be careful about what kind of energy you put out into the world! Any negative energy you produce has a ripple effect, affecting others, maybe even people you don't even know.

What's your sign?

Don't forget that according to Chinese astrology, certain signs are more compatible with others. The zodiac can definitely affect your working relationships. If you're a Snake and your boss is a Tiger, look out! The Snake and the Tiger are two of the least compatible signs in the Chinese horoscope.

Understanding your sign may at least help you recognize that you may have to put forth a very special effort to get along with a difficult or incompatible sign. See Chapter 1 for more information about Chinese astrology.

Putting in some chi before me

The presence of the people who occupied your workspace before you may affect your workspace's energy. That *predecessor chi,* be it positive or negative, affects you on a subtle level, so "seeing" it is difficult. You may intuit that the overhead beam is oppressing you, but your eyesight can't tell you that your predecessor left behind some unhappy atmosphere.

You have to rely on intuition to detect negative predecessor chi. For example, you may feel slightly uncomfortable but can't pinpoint the cause of your discomfort. If you've been in a workspace for a while, have introduced the principles of Feng Shui to it, and *still* feel some subtle negative energy, it may be predecessor chi. If Feng Shui cures in your workspace aren't as successful as they could be this may indicate negative predecessor chi.

To determine more about predecessor chi, find out about the people who worked in the space you're about to move into (or now occupy). Ask questions about how they did their work, whether they liked their job, and what happened when they left. If they enjoyed their work, you'll get beneficial energy. If they disliked the job, look out. Although predecessor chi stretches back to the very first person that occupied the space you're in now, the most important is the predecessor who was in the space immediately before you. Investigating before you take over a space can help anticipate if you'll need to cure the space. If the predecessor chi is extremely negative, it may convince you to ask for a different desk.

In a work environment, generally, Table 14-1's guidelines hold.

Freeing chi via ceremony

To ensure positive energy in your workspace, you may want to perform a blessing ceremony. This is real, hard-core Feng Shui, but there's no need to become a Buddhist if you're not one already. A *blessing ceremony* is simply a way of inviting abundance into your life, clearing negative energy from your environment and improving your own energy. In other words, a blessing ceremony is similar to setting your intentions.

Remember to respect your co-workers and how they might feel about the ceremony, which they may perceive as religious. If necessary, perform the ceremony after hours or on a weekend. If they seem open to it, invite them to join you in creating positive energy in your workspace.

As you perform the ceremony, keep your intentions firmly in mind. If you feel the need, you can dress in your Feng Shui best . . . but you can leave the Bagua-embroidered robe at home.

The Orange Peel Blessing works inside a building to enhance positive chi.

1. Gather nine oranges and a deep bowl.

2. Take a few moments to relax.

    Clear your mind and take a few deep breaths.

3. Recite an intention nine times (nine being an auspicious number).

4. Fill the bowl about halfway with water.

5. Peel the oranges.

    Use only the peels. (Make a fruit salad with the fruit itself.)

6. Add the peels to the water.

7. Starting at the entrance to your workspace or office, sprinkle a small amount of the water.

    Visualize good energy sweeping away and replacing all the negative energy.

8. Walk throughout your workspace, sprinkling water, and saying your mantra or intention.

    Use care and consideration and clean up any spilled water or areas where the water may cause slips.

9. End where you started.

    No need to use all the water. Discard the remaining water and peels in your garden, if you have one. Otherwise, the water goes down the drain and the peels in the compost pile.

Table 14-1	Predecessor Chi Left for Thee
Why she's gone	**What kind of energy you're gonna get**
She was promoted.	Beneficial
She was demoted.	Negative
She was fired.	Negative
She left because of disability, disease, or death.	Negative
She got a different job.	Neutral

Counteract negative predecessor chi with these ideas:

- ✔ **Place your intentions.** See Chapter 1 for more information.

- ✔ **Use your good, positive energy.** It can help you overcome the negative chi in the space.

- ✔ **Use traditional Feng Shui cures.** Chose from fountains, aquariums, wind chimes, mirrors, and crystals. Chapter 16 talks more about these.

- ✔ **Perform a blessing ceremony.** See "Freeing chi via ceremony" sidebar in this chapter for details on the ceremony.

If possible, don't work in a space with strong negative predecessor chi. See if you can be assigned to a more positive (or even neutral) workspace.

Spotlighting the Relationship and Helpful People Sectors

Two Life Sectors in the Bagua are primarily responsible for your relationships at work: The Relationship sector and the Helpful People sector. Of course, these two sectors have some overlap, and you want to pay attention to both of them in order to create the best opportunities for career success.

By paying attention to the Bagua's Relationship and Helpful People sectors, you're telling yourself — and the world — that other people matter to you, and that's powerful medicine! As you work to balance

Feng Shui elements in these areas or add cures to enhance the chi in them, be certain to deliberately and thoughtfully set your intentions. Say something like, "Because I know that getting along well with others will help my career, and create more personal happiness and joy, I place this crystal in the Relationship sector to show my intention to do my best to get along with others, to heal relationships that aren't healthy, and to treat others with respect and consideration."

If the Relationship sector or the Helpful People sector is missing in your workspace or your desk, hurry up and find it. Otherwise, you may have problems with your co-workers, boss, and clients. In other words, your career may be in big trouble! You need a symbolic cure. (Think mirrors, crystals, Feng Shui fountains, and the like.)

To see where to enhance the chi in your environment, place the Bagua over a template of your workspace and/or your desk with the south or Fame sector located at the entrance to your workspace. (On your desk, the "entrance" is where your chair "enters" the desk.)

Relationship sector

When applied to a work environment, the Relationship sector influences your relationships with everyone. The sector influences your relationships with everyone from your boss to the person in the next cubicle. The Relationship sector is the Southwest sector.

To raise the chi, try these ideas:

- ✔ Place a photograph of people who love you or support you in your career in the Relationship sector.

- ✔ Enhance the Earth element in the Relationship sector. (Earth is the element associated with this sector.) Add an object that symbolizes the earth or a color associated with the Earth element.

- ✔ Crystals empower. A rock formation or crystal (Earth element) can be a strong cure for the Relationship sector.

Don't forget to give back! Giving back creates powerful positive chi, too. If you have the chance to do a co-worker a favor and be a Helpful Person, then do it. Never forget that relationships are reciprocal. It's the old principle of Karma . . . What goes around, comes around!

Want some ethics with your coffee?

Conducting business in an ethical way is very good Feng Shui! *Ethics* is about how you conduct yourself with others. If you behave in a trustworthy way, then you're not abusing other people's trust and confidence in you. Benevolent blessings and abundance will flow toward you!

Some companies have codes of ethics their employees are expected to practice. Others have company cultures that emphasize behaving ethically, even if the code isn't written down. Although a company's leaders need to set the ethical tone, every individual, no matter what his or her job, is responsible for behaving ethically at work.

When applying ethics to the workplace, remember

✔ Ethics are based on personal standards of behavior. Set your standards high!

✔ Be consistent. If it's not ethical to lie to a client, it's not ethical to lie to a co-worker.

✔ Use your ethical code to guide all your decisions and actions.

✔ Resist unethical practices among co-workers, clients, and others by stating your position clearly. If something can't stand the scrutiny of daylight — if you can't discuss it openly — it probably isn't ethical or something you want your name associated with.

Helpful People sector

The Helpful People sector influences those people who can help you in one way or another — the boss who approves a promotion for you, the client whose praise helps you flourish in your career, or the co-worker who offers helpful advice on an important project. The Helpful People sector is the Northwest sector.

To raise the chi in Helpful People, try these ideas:

✔ Enhance the Metal element in the Helpful People sector (Metal is the element associated with this sector). Add a metal picture frame or a white object to the sector.

✔ Pot a plant in a metal container. The plant, placed in the Relationship or Helping People sector, enhances both sectors because Earth supports Metal in the Nourishing Cycle of the Five Elements.

✔ Crystals empower, so add a crystal to this sector to enhance the chi.

According to Feng Shui, Helpful People make abundance come to you. Thus, the Helpful People sector is related to the Wealth sector. So if you want to see your wealth increase (both literally and metaphorically), pay attention to the Helpful People sector!

You can raise the chi in the Wealth sector. Wood is the element associated with Wealth, so enhance this element to enhance the positive energy in your wealth sector. Add colors associated with Wood or wood objects to the sector. Or try one of these cures:

✔ Place a metal bowl filled with coins in your Wealth sector. See Chapter 17 for more information.

✔ Hang a gourd in your Wealth sector. *Gourds,* which are hard-rined fruits related to squash, are full of seeds that symbolically represent abundance. Small gourds can be purchased at farmers' markets and at some grocery stores in the fall. Hang them by gluing or tying a string to the stem.

✔ Put a fountain in the Wealth area. Water symbolizes abundance.

Mother Nature, can you take a memo?

One of the most important relationships you have is the one you have with Mother Nature. Honoring the Earth, which nurtures and gives life to all living creatures, isn't only good Feng Shui, it's plain common sense.

The principles of Feng Shui show that using natural objects is healthier and more favorable for everyone. Throughout this book, we encourage you to choose natural materials instead of artificial ones.

In your workspace, we also encourage you to develop an environmental consciousness by taking the following steps.

✔ Reduce the number of toxic chemicals you rely on.

✔ Start a recycling program.

✔ Cut down on waste — use a ceramic coffee mug instead of Styrofoam cups. Do your best to honor your Mother!

Cultivating helpful people — just add a few seeds

Be aware that helpful people come in all shapes and sizes. Therefore, treat every-one with kindness and respect, apologize when it's called for, and withhold assump-tions and judgmental thinking. Just because you're the Really, Really Important High-Up in the Hierarchy Person doesn't mean you're allowed to treat the secre-tary rudely. In fact, if you do, you may find it difficult to have your messages relayed to the Even More Important Higher-Up in the Hierarchy Person.

In addition to enhancing the chi in your desk and/or workspace's Helpful People sector, you can cultivate Helpful People by never underestimating the power of sin-cerity. If you present yourself as a person who is open to new ideas, interested in others, and not merely out for your own gain, you'll attract helpful people. If you're insincere, however, others recognize your insincerity and may actually avoid help-ing you! No matter how hard you try, you can't fake sincerity.

Chapter 15

Making Your To-Do List: Meeting Goals

*I*n this chapter, we show you how to take charge not just of your workspace but also of your work! In previous chapters, we give you information on how Feng Shui can benefit you, if you apply its principles to your workspace. Now, we also show how to apply Feng Shui to your *life* so that you can achieve greater career success. (Yes, indeed, you can apply interior design philosophy to how you live your life!)

Feng Shui is about living a balanced, harmonious life, setting goals (intentions), and achieving them. This chapter describes how taking action can help you get what you want from life through Feng Shui. We show you how taking control, remaining positive, setting goals and even dressing the Feng Shui way can all contribute to your career success.

Choosing Control: You Have More Power Than You Think

Unless you're independently wealthy, you probably have to work for a living. That means going to your job (and staying there), even on the days when you have a headache, the boss asks you to run out and buy a birthday present for his dog, and every customer who walks through the door is singing "Yes, I Have No Bananas." You want to walk away, but the rent is due and your 10-year-old needs braces. Under these circumstances, you can easily feel powerless and downtrodden — and it's no big surprise that many people do.

But instead of feeling powerless about your work (and your life), choose assertiveness and empowerment. You have more power — control, energy and influence — than you think. Use the principles of Feng Shui to start taking control over your working life and exerting power over your career. Although you don't have control over everything that happens in your life (or your career), you do have control over how you feel, how you react, and how you plan for the future.

To take charge of your work and career, you need to start by changing your perceptions. Then you can take action. Start with the following steps to get going on the right track:

1. **Ask yourself *why* you're doing what you're doing.**

   Why do I want more career success?

   Why do I want more wealth?

   What do I hope to achieve by taking control?

2. **Make a commitment to be mindful.**

   Whenever you feel doubt or question your path . . . go back and ask yourself why you're doing what you're doing. If you can't figure this out, you have some thinking to do!

3. **Decide to create positive energy in the world.**

   Negative energy can come from the stressed-out, down-in-the-dumps, complaining-about-every-little-thing attitude everyone displays sometimes. The goal is not to display it very often! This is such an important aspect of gaining power and control that we devote an entire section to it later in the chapter. (See "Being Upbeat before You Beat Someone Up: Positivity at Work.")

4. **Believe in yourself.**

   If you don't believe in yourself, how can you trust yourself to be in control and be effective? Each day is a fresh start. See "Powering Up Intentions with Positive Affirmations," later in this chapter for more information about bolstering your confidence.

Being Upbeat Before You Beat Someone Up: Positivity at Work

To create positive energy, you need to maintain a positive outlook about your work. A positive outlook is a mindset more than any-thing else — you can either grumble and groan about the copier malfunctioning just when you need it, or you can decide that having to run over to the neighborhood copy center gives you a chance to stretch your legs and get out in the sun. You can choose to have a positive outlook regardless of circumstances, or you can choose to have a negative outlook (also regardless of circum-stances). We think it's healthier (and more fun) to choose a positive outlook.

Maintaining a positive outlook at work involves four strategies:

✔ **Deciding to be positive.** This decision is the single most important you'll ever make! If putting only positive energy out into the world seems a bit of a stretch (you are only human), start with a few simple approaches:

- **Resist the temptation to play the complaining game.** When everyone else is moaning about the new boss, don't join them. Figure out a way to get along with the new boss.

- **For one day, be courteous and polite to all the people you encounter.** Do so whether they deserve it or not, from the obnoxious co-worker in the next cubicle to the rude waiter at the downtown café. After you see how choosing not to react to impoliteness or minor annoy-ances can improve your mood and attitude, you'll proba-bly want to keep doing it! (If one day is too much to start with, then do it for one morning or even one hour!)

- **Take a deep breath and stop yourself before making a criticism.** The criticism may be valid, and you may have to make it, but stop and think before you do.

- **Express your pleasure in the world.** If a co-worker's necklace is gorgeous, go ahead and say so. If you think the spring flowers in the front of the building look spectacular, mention it to the next person you see.

✔ **Enjoying and taking pleasure in what you do.** No one loves every single aspect about his or her job, but you should have a strong element of pleasure in what you do. If not, maybe you need a career change (or at least a job change), additional training, or maybe just an attitude adjustment.

✔ **Focusing on the goals needed for career success.** If you're a cashier at a local discount store, then being consistently polite and pleasant to customers is a key behavior. Don't focus on the fact that your feet hurt after standing on them all day, or that you can hardly wait for your shift to be over. Focusing on the wrong things can make your job harder and won't improve your chances of being promoted to head cashier.

✔ **Staying present-oriented and aware.** Instead of counting the minutes until quitting time (what a waste of precious hours!), focus on the present. Even if your work is, at the moment, mundane and boring, be present and do it well. If you look at your work with the right frame of mind, mundane and boring work can give you an opportunity to empty your mind and relax, or to think about a problem or a challenge you're having in your life and to brainstorm possible solutions.

Surrounding yourself with what you love

The principles of Feng Shui teach that you should surround yourself with objects that fulfill their function effectively, and that bring you pleasure. Having objects you love in your workspace is one of the best ways we know to help you maintain a positive outlook during the eight or ten hours you're at your desk.

Including artwork in your workspace — whether it's a picture on the wall or a small statue for your desktop — can help you feel good about your environment. Investing some time and money in finding a good piece or two of art can pay dividends!

People are often utilitarian with their workspaces. They need a container for their pens, so they buy the plastic one for two dollars at the office supply store. In order to bring some Fire element onto your desktop, you decide to get a red container.

But before you hop over to the nearest office supply store to buy a red plastic penholder, consider these other options:

✔ Bring in the red coffee mug you bought on that last vacation. Every time you look at it, you'll have warm memories and good feelings.

✔ Buy an unpainted wooden box and paint it with red motifs this weekend, allowing your creativity free reign. Every time you look at it, you'll feel inspired by your creative genius.

✔ Do an art project with your kids, with the result being a container for your pens. Every time you look at it, you'll remember the time you spent together making it with your little ones.

Smelling good when your day stinks: Aromatherapy and music

Maintaining a positive outlook can be difficult when you're having a tough day at work. Sometimes being near objects that you love most doesn't seem to help. For times like these, Feng Shui has some practical answers:

Introduce aromatherapy and music into your workspace.

Putting on some tunes

We don't mean heavy metal or rap music. We're talking about classical music, nature music, and New Age music — the type of music that can be played low in the background, is appealing to listen to, and can help you relax. Enya's music is especially lovely and appeals to both men and women looking for tranquil background music.

Some people find that having a CD or radio playing soft music all day long helps them accomplish their work and camouflages otherwise irritating and distracting noises in their environment. Others don't care to listen all day long, but find that putting a CD on every now and then helps them relax and de-stress. See Chapter 4 for more about sound.

Taking a whiff

Aromatherapy can be a terrific pick-me-up. You can have fragrance in your office all the time by

✔ Placing a bowl of potpourri near your desk. Stirring it occasionally helps freshen the fragrance.

✔ Spraying fragrance spritzers around your office.

✔ Making your own aromatherapy scents by diluting essential oils with water or mineral oil.

✔ Burning fragrant candles and incense. People who work from home (or those with very understanding bosses) can do this.

✔ Wearing your own personal fragrance. If you don't like to wear perfume, cologne, or aftershave, try lightly scented hand lotion or soaps that leave a lingering scent.

Table 15-1 reveals some great scents and what they do.

Table 15-1   Aromashui: Scents and Their Sensibilities

Scent	What it does
Citrus orange	Invigorates and freshens your space with great chi.
Lavender	Helps you relax; helps drivers stay alert yet calm and have a feeling of security.
Rosemary and lemon	Especially good for helping drivers remain calm and attentive.
Cinnamon or clove	Helps you focus.
Pine	Fosters patience.
Peppermint	Counteracts indecision and helps keep you awake.

Use essential oils carefully, remembering to always dilute them if applying directly to your skin and not pointing them in any unsafe direction (like your eyes or prized cashmere sweater). Also, check with your co-workers before bringing scents to work — some people may be sensitive or allergic to strong scents. And remember to be especially careful before burning candles and incense. Get permission and use extra caution, as this can be dangerous.

Establishing Your Professional Goals and Setting Career Intentions

The lessons of Feng Shui can help you enhance your career in a number of different ways. Although ancient Feng Shui masters didn't have the same career concerns that you may have, they understood the power of the human mind for shaping lives. Don't underestimate the power of your own mind!

Feng Shui teaches the power of intention. By being clear about what you intend to do, you make a commitment to yourself to do it. Setting your intentions is about understanding what you're doing, why you're doing it, and how you're going to do it.

Getting to your goals

Of course, you can't become your company's CEO purely through the power of positive thinking, just as you can't raise the chi in your workspace merely by thinking about throwing away all that clutter (you actually have to throw away the clutter first).

In order to achieve career success, you need to decide what your goals are, make a plan for meeting them, and use the power of intention (through the use of affirmations, later in this chapter) to help you achieve them. Remember, you can't have meaningful intentions without also having goals related to those intentions.

Set your goals high. Keep high expectations for yourself in your career and at work. If you sometimes fail to meet these lofty standards, you'll still be achieving far beyond the rest of the crowd.

To reach your goals you must devise a plan. This plan consists of the steps to take to achieve your goal. After you have a goal that meets good goal-setting criteria (see the sidebar, "Creating goals you can achieve"), you can create a plan toward achieving the goal.

Powering up intentions with positive affirmations

When you make an intention in Feng Shui, you say something like, "I am placing this crystal on my desk to enhance the good energy in my Career sector so that my career success will be improved. By doing this, I am making a commitment to succeeding in my career."

That type of intention is extremely effective But another type of intention is equally as effective — affirmations. An *affirmation* is simply an intention you want to achieve stated as if you've already achieved it. This process of visualizing and believing in your goals helps you to achieve them.

Instead of saying, "I want to lose 30 pounds," which may be a reasonable intention, an affirmation says, "I am a slender and healthy person," even if you're, ahem, a little on the plump side.

Creating goals you can achieve

To successfully achieve your goals, you need to spell out exactly what they are and how you know when you've achieved them. The following criteria can help you create achievable goals. Make your goals

✔ Specific. You should know exactly what you're trying to achieve. For example, a work-related goal may be, "I will finish in the top ten in sales at the end of this quarter." You will know whether you were in the top ten or not.

✔ Measurable. Saying, "My goal is to be a top-selling salesperson" isn't easily measured. Make the measurement plain: "I will sell 50,000 widgets this year." You can easily measure whether you sold 50,000 widgets or not by the end of the year.

✔ Have a specific time frame. Saying, "I will sell 50,000 widgets" is meaningless unless you give it a time frame. Will you sell that many widgets this month, this year, in your career?

✔ Be challenging but realistic. If you've never sold more than 10 widgets in a month, setting a goal to sell 100 of them in a month is unrealistic. A more realistic — and more attainable goal — is to challenge yourself to sell 12 or 15 widgets in a month.

✔ Include a mix of short-term and long-term goals. Long-term goals focus on where you see yourself and your career in five years or ten years (or longer). Short-term goals include what you hope to achieve within six months or so.

✔ Limited in number. Set one or two long-term goals and perhaps two or three short-term goals. Otherwise, you won't know where to focus your energy because all the competing goals will distract you.

Re-evaluate your goals regularly. Revisit your long-term goals yearly, and re-examine your short-term goals according to the length of time you have to accomplish them. You may look at a six-month goal every two weeks or month. By examining your goals as you move toward reaching them, you can decide if you're making good progress, if you need to modify the goals, and if you're still committed to the same goals.

The power of affirmations is that the more you tell yourself a message, the more your mind believes it.

So if the message you send to yourself is that you're slender and healthy, you're much more likely to act like a slender and healthy person (for example, by eating better and working out more) than if you're constantly telling yourself, "You're an overweight, unlovable creature who will never amount to anything."

Repeat affirmations daily until they're so firmly a part of your belief system you accept them without question. Often, people post a list of their affirmations where they see them regularly.

As you create and set your work affirmations, keep in mind the following guidelines:

- ✔ Focus your affirmations at work on work-related topics only: "I am an approachable CEO who listens to all my employees," or "I am an award-winning customer service representative."

- ✔ Limit your affirmations to three or four of the most important, most powerful intentions you have. After you achieve them, add new affirmations.

- ✔ Post affirmations on a wall or in a desk drawer where you see them frequently.

- ✔ Briefly reaffirm the affirmations every time you see them.

- ✔ Tell yourself your affirmations every time you arrive at work.

- ✔ Re-think your affirmations, change them as needed, and recommit yourself to them every few months.

To further empower your results, you can write your affirmations on red paper, or place in a frame with a red mat. Writing your affirmations in a bold script will reinforce your commitment to the changes you're up for in your work and your life. Be creative and add touches such as black lettering outlined in gold.

To emphasize your commitment even more, as you speak your affirmations you might consider looking into a mirror that alerts you to people traffic behind you at your desk. Focus on the words and your intention, not the color of your lipstick.

Dressing for Success

Feng Shui can also show you how to dress for success. By using Feng Shui principles in your dress, you can start each morning focusing on your goals, intentions, and affirmations. As you put on your green scarf signifying the Wood element, you can tell yourself that you're taking steps to achieve career success. Personal Feng Shui — actually wearing objects that have a symbolic meaning in Feng Shui — is an effective way to take Feng Shui with you wherever you go.

In Chapters 9 and 12, we talk about how some people don't have regular workspaces that they go to each day to work. We suggest that these people wear their Feng Shui. Even if you do have a workspace you go to every day, you can also enhance your career success by wearing your Feng Shui. If you work in corporate America, wearing a suit embroidered with waves to increase your Water element may not be a good idea, but there *are* practical steps that you can take.

Picking out a Feng Shui getup

Remember that each Life Sector has colors and elements associated with it. And keep in mind that Feng Shui cures (such as crystals) work whether you hang them from the ceiling or from your wrist. By deciding what sector you want to enhance, you can find a corresponding wardrobe item to raise the chi in that sector.

Crystals can enhance the chi in a Life Sector. Apply that knowledge to your personal wardrobe, and you'll see that if you wear a crystal — perhaps in a bracelet or on a chain — you can raise your personal chi!

Suppose you're trying to enhance your Fame sector. You know that red, the color of the Fire element, is the color associated with Fame. Now, you don't have to run out and buy a red suit (especially if you're a man), but you can certainly wear a red scarf or a red tie.

Don't forget that a whole spectrum of color exists! If bright red doesn't suit you, consider burgundy, which has the same power as red. Even pink is, for Feng Shui purposes, a version of red. So if you've just found a hot pink pocket protector, go ahead and wear it with pride.

Don't feel you have to wear red just because that enhances the Fame sector and you want to be famous. If black suits you better, then wear black!

Feng Shui chic

Remember how we keep encouraging you to choose objects you love? The same goes for your wardrobe. Wear personal objects that you love. In addition to your actual clothes, think jewelry, belts, ties, and scarves . . . even wallets and handbags can make a Feng Shui statement.

Holly wears the same crystal bracelet every day because of the good feelings it gives her. When giving a Feng Shui consultation, she wears a special hand painted silk scarf with designs of yin and yang, the Bagua, and the words of a blessing around the border.

See Figure 15-1 for an example of personal Feng Shui.

Figure 15-1: Holly wears a special blue scarf to encourage focus and clear communication.

Dressing up your intentions

Setting intentions as you place cures helps the cures work. The same principle applies to your dress. Consciously thinking or speaking your intentions as you dress each day can help you feel more powerful at work. As you clip on your crystal earrings, you can tell yourself, "By wearing these crystals, I will be enhancing the chi wherever I go. I will bring good energy and a positive outlook with me throughout the day." Think how powerful that is!

You can communicate your intentions through your dress in other ways. For example:

- ✔ Create a wardrobe filled with clothing that looks good on you and that makes you feel comfortable and confident.

- ✔ Make certain your clothing is always clean, pressed, and in good repair.

- ✔ Choose clothing that communicates your style.

- ✔ Dress professionally instead of relying only on casual clothes.

✔ Understand why you're wearing what you're wearing. For example, blue is the color that corresponds to clear communication. Holly chooses blue for clarity because when she gives talks and seminars, she needs to be certain the audience understands her message and takes away specific, helpful information.

You can have too much of a good thing. Remember to avoid clutter when deciding what to wear, while still maintaining your personal style and flair. For example Holly is small in stature and she chooses her jewelry carefully, usually focusing on great earrings and her crystal bracelet. Too much jewelry feels cluttered and overdressed to her. The same goes with color and style of clothing. In order to feel empowered and raise your personal chi, spend time getting in touch with what makes you feel best, and you can't go wrong!

Part V
The Part of Tens

"I assume everyone on your team is on board with the proposed changes to the office layout."

In this part . . .

If you want to jump-start your career and need to do it now, then this is the section for you! We whipped up some top ten lists for quick reference. Find out how to cure common workplace problems, pick up hints on how to increase your wealth, discover ways to create harmony with your co-workers (yes, even the annoying ones), and find out how to get yourself into a power position — all the Feng Shui way.

Chapter 16

Ten Top Feng Shui Helpers

In This Chapter

▶ De-cluttering your space
▶ Setting intentions with purpose
▶ Choosing cures to place

*F*eng Shui uses *cures* — simple objects that raise or enhance the chi in an area — to overcome design challenges and to enhance the chi in your environment.

If you haven't read all the chapters, then pay close attention. If your office environment isn't as warm and welcoming as it could be, Feng Shui cures can help you make that workspace warmer, more supportive, and more welcoming. The ten most effective cures you can use to solve Feng Shui challenges in your workspace follow.

Clearing the Floor, Clearing Your Mind

We can't emphasize enough that keeping your workspace clutter-free is the first step to solving the world's problems. Or at least your workspace challenges.

Keeping your space clutter-free isn't, unfortunately, a one-time deal. You have to keep at it. For that reason, you need to have a system in place that helps you deal with the clutter before it becomes clutter and blocks the free flow of chi throughout your workspace.

Placing Cures with Intention

We can't overstate the power of intentions, even though we've tried. Whenever you set a cure in place or choose an object that represents one of the Five Elements, tell yourself what the meaning of the cure or object is. Say, "By placing this pyramid-shaped crystal, which represents the Fire Element, in the Fame sector of my desk, I will enhance my reputation in the company and improve my career outlook."

By saying what you want and stating your intentions out loud — as long as your co-workers don't give you funny looks — you tell yourself — and the universe — what you want. If you don't know what you want, even Feng Shui can't get it for you.

Bringing in the Bagua

The octagonal shape of the Bagua is a powerful symbol. Adding objects shaped like the Bagua to your workspace can raise the chi in your workspace and in all Life Sectors. You can choose Bagua-shaped mirrors (they come in all sizes). You can choose an object, such as a box, that has eight sides. If you're creative, you can make an eight-sided textile to hang on the wall.

Color Me Beautiful

Color is a powerful way to bring balance into your workspace. You can use color to enhance yin or yang energy in a room. In other words, if your workspace has you bouncing off walls, you can soothe the action with yin colors. If, on the other hand, you want to nap at your desk every afternoon, add a little zesty yang color. See Chapter 5 for more information about adding color.

Color also represents the Five Elements, so if you need to add Wood Element to your space, you can use an object in the hue of green. Colors are also related to Life Sectors on the Bagua, so if you need to enhance your Career sector, a little something blue or black is a good idea.

Mixing in Some Music

Adding music to your workspace can make it more inviting. Music can also help disguise the racket that takes place in a typical office.

You can choose wind chimes that make a gentle, pleasing sound as someone walks by, or you can play a CD of relaxing classical music.

Don't forget, though, that what is music to your ears may not be music to your co-workers. Respect them and keep the volume turned low or better yet, use headphones.

Using Your Schnoz

Fragrances and scents can serve as a wonderful pick-me-up as you work at your desk. When appropriate, you can

- ✔ Burn some incense.
- ✔ Carry and use a spritzer bottle of aromatic oils.
- ✔ Keep a bowl of potpourri open on a shelf.

Like music, strong fragrances and scents can be distracting to your co-workers, especially those with allergies. Check with your co-workers to see if they mind, and ask your boss if your company allows you to burn candles or incense.

Working Around Water

The sound of water trickling over rocks in a fountain makes a natural music that can be quite soothing. The mesmerizing movement of fish swimming around and around in an aquarium can be relaxing. A water fountain or aquarium enhances the Water Element in your workspace. It helps to raise the chi and can make clients and co-workers feel relaxed and welcome.

Crystallizing Your Thoughts

Crystals (transparent quartz stones available in gift stores and New Age shops) can raise the chi in your workspace and can make up for missing areas of the Bagua. If you have a Feng Shui challenge, such as a column in your office that may send cutting chi your way, hanging a crystal near the column can solve the problem. If your workspace is an odd shape and a Life Sector is missing, a crystal hung near the missing area symbolically completes the Bagua.

Reflecting and Deflecting Chi: Mirrors

You can use mirrors to enhance good chi and to deflect negative chi. A Bagua mirror hung over your front door or the entrance to your workspace can prevent negative chi from entering. If you want to enhance the chi in a certain Life Sector, you can place a mirror there. Or, if a sector of the Bagua is missing in your workspace, a mirror placed near the affected area can symbolically complete it.

 Don't use an outdoors Bagua mirror, with its I Ching symbols, on an inside office door. You can use an eight-sided mirror, which is auspicious, but don't use the special Bagua mirror with the trigram symbols.

Planting Your Intentions

Plants enhance chi — and they're also gorgeous to look at. Plants can enhance the Wood and Earth Elements in your workspace. By selecting a plant with colored blossoms, you can add a nice color cure. You can combine various elements with plants. For example, a nice brass planter for your plant adds the Metal Element to your workspace without the addition of another object. Plants should be alive, healthy, and round-leaved.

Chapter 17

Ten Ways to Increase Your Wealth

● ●

In This Chapter

▶ Setting your intentions

▶ Finding the Wealth sector

▶ Remembering to say thanks

● ●

*W*e know that many readers are probably interested in the contents of this chapter. After all, who couldn't use a bit more spending money? In this chapter, we focus on simple yet powerful ways that you can use Feng Shui in your workspace to increase your wealth.

Wealth doesn't have to mean cold hard cash, so those of you who are on a more highly evolved plane and are ready to skip to the next chapter may want to read a bit further. Wealth, in Feng Shui terms, simply means abundance. It means having a sufficiency of whatever you want, whether it's love or good health or kids or . . . a bank account in Switzerland. Wealth also is the inner knowledge that your heart is filled with riches.

Also realize that Feng Shui isn't magic. If you want to increase the amount of money you make, you're going to have to work at it. Feng Shui can help improve your chances of success, but it won't give you the winning lottery numbers. Especially if you never buy a ticket.

Knowing What You Want

In order to get what you want, you have to know what you want. If you want to increase your wealth — and by wealth you mean money — then acknowledge that and say, as you set your cures, that what you want is more financial strength. Also figure out why you want more money. Is it so you can provide for your family or so you can buy that chateau in Lorraine? Feng Shui doesn't care, but you need to know what you're aiming for in order to get it.

Giving the Wealth Sector a Nod

Using a Bagua, find the Wealth sector of your workspace and/or your desktop. Finding this sector and raising the chi in it is the place to begin. This sector is extremely important to creating abundance in your life.

The *mouth of chi,* the door to your cubicle or office, determines your Wealth sector. You can find your Wealth sector in the far-left corner of the room from your door.

Achieving the abundance you desire can be a challenge if the Wealth sector is missing in your workspace or desktop. This happens because the room or desk is irregularly shaped. Using cures can help, as can getting a raise.

Pushing the Envelope

In traditional Feng Shui, a red envelope signifies the conduit or protective sleeve for money (or any token of appreciation) when you offer payment in thanks for Feng Shui advice. The red envelope protects the chi of the master giving the cure and is considered a must with many Feng Shui practitioners. Placing a red envelope in the Wealth sector symbolically creates abundance for you (and may literally create abundance, too!) Remember to set your intention as you place the envelope.

Red envelopes are also used during Chinese New Year celebrations. They're very appropriate when giving gifts to business friends or associates symbolizing the good fortune to come in the New Year. They can be purchased at some specialty stationery shops and in some New Age stores.

Cashing In on Desk Placement

Placing your desk in a powerful position helps bring money your way. Your desk's power position is the direction in which your desk faces the door (or your workspace's entrance) but isn't directly opposite the door. Your back should be to a wall so that you're supported energetically from behind. Try to have a clear, wide view of your work area.

Welcoming Chi

Allowing the chi to come into your workspace and move freely around is one key to increasing abundance. Don't allow anything to block your workspace's doorway or entrance (one good reason to keep your door open at least part of the day).

Use your "Feng Shui eyes" to keep your workspace free of clutter and arrange your furniture so that chi can move freely about the space. Following these simple guidelines gives you a more confident and grounded feeling as you work.

Dishing Up Some Coins

A traditional Chinese cure to increase abundance is to place a metal dish with coins in your Wealth sector (on your desk is the perfect place). Some people like to use Chinese coins, but this is not necessary. The coins don't bring you luck so much as they reinforce your intention to increase the abundance in your life. Every time you see the coins, you remember, "Aha! One of my goals is to increase my wealth . . . so maybe I should finish those reports and keep my job."

Planting Your Money Tree

Healthy plant life in the Wealth sector gives benevolent chi in that area a boost. Use a simple lush plant in a small pot on your desk-top, or a larger tree-like *ficus benjimina* in the Wealth corner of your office. A Venus' flytrap is probably one to avoid.

If living plants aren't your thing, select a lovely silk plant, (although we recommend a live one if at all possible).

Lighting Your Wealth Life

Lighting makes a powerful chi enhancer for your Wealth sector. Use a simple indirect uplight, such as a torchier lamp. Traditional floor lamps also work well, as do pole lamps with cans. Be creative and see how you can experiment with alternative, decorator lighting. Even pillar candles or an elegant candelabra in your Wealth area can have an excellent effect. Chapter 4 sheds some more light on this topic.

"Wetting" Your Appetite

The use of gently moving water in the Wealth area is used frequently to raise the chi. Try a simple fountain, with the water directed inward toward (never away from) you. The water needs to be kept fresh and sparkling at all times. A few drops of chlorine every month takes care of any algae buildup. Fountains can be a simple tabletop type that sits on a pedestal, or other flat surface, such as a filing cabinet or bookcase.

Enhancing Chi with Crystals

Crystals can be powerful chi boosters. Crystals positioned in the Wealth sector can greatly enhance the chi. Remember to keep them clean and dust free. When first acquiring your crystal, try to cleanse it in the ocean, a clear stream, river, or other natural source of fresh water. If you can't easily find any other pure water, you can use distilled water.

You can further enhance the chi of your earth crystal by placing it on an octagonal, Bagua-shaped mirror usually found in gift or craft shops. You can hang the faceted type with fishing line for a "floating" look, or a red string for a more traditional Feng Shui application.

Honoring Your Helpful People

We can't leave this chapter without the mention of the Helpful People who are our clients, customers, and supportive patrons. The Helpful People sector on the Bagua is positioned diagonally across from the Wealth sector. This location is a strong indicator that these two areas are energetically linked and each has a powerful impact on the other. Treat people the way you want to be treated, and do them one better. You won't regret it. Following this mantra is good Feng Shui.

Chapter 18

Ten Ways to Create Harmony with Co-Workers

*I*f you have a job, you have co-workers — or at least a boss, or clients, or someone — with whom you must maintain friendly relations if you want to keep your job, remain productive, and/or get paid.

If everyone were as nice, pleasant, cooperative, and timely as you are, keeping friendly relationships with your co-workers, boss, and clients wouldn't be difficult. But unfortunately, you don't work in never-never land and you sometimes have co-workers who aren't so easy to get along with. But never fear Feng Shui is here. You can use the principles of Feng Shui to enhance your relationships with those people who are important in your business. Use these top ten strategies:

Having Honorable Intentions

Do we sound like we're repeating ourselves? You say we actually are repeating ourselves? Well, vital information deserves to be emphasized.

You can't have happy relationships with your co-workers just by enhancing the Relationship sector of your office and then ignoring all the junior employees. You have to decide that you want better relations with your co-workers, and you have to commit to doing your share to ensure that you aren't the cause of unhappy feelings.

(We know, you would *never* be the cause of unhappy feelings. This tip is for the other readers.)

Finding the Bagua's Co-worker Sector

Surprise! You don't find a Co-worker sector on the Bagua. But you can find a Marriage sector (and while you're at work, this sector rules your relationships with your co-workers, boss, and clients). You also find a Helpful People sector, which includes bosses, co-workers, and clients — even janitors — who can help enhance your career. Locate these two sectors in your workspace and/or on your desktop, and enhance the chi by adding mirrors, crystals, a loved object, or something symbolic of one of the Five Elements. Enhancing the chi in these sectors will improve your relationships with others.

If one of these sectors is missing from your workspace or desk, you may have more difficulty in your relationships, and you need to pay particular attention to symbolically completing the missing area. Use a cure, such as a mirror or crystal, to raise the chi and complete the area. See Chapter 1 for further information.

Enhancing Elemental Essentials

The Metal element enhances the Helpful People sector. The use of the Earth element augments the Relationship sector. By adding objects that symbolize either of these elements to your workspace, especially to its related sector, you can help improve your relationship with co-workers. (Remember to set your intention.)

Examples of the Earth element are brick or terra-cotta tiles or ceramic figures; rocks and stones also represent the Earth element. Coins and metal objects, such as brass plant containers, symbolize the Metal element.

Sticking in Shapely Elements

The shape associated with the Earth element is the square, and the shape associated with the Metal element is the circle. By adding square or circular objects to the Helpful People or Relationship sector, you can help keep relationships with your co-workers on an even keel. If you place a square ceramic container in the

Relationship sector, you're combining two aspects of the Earth element and therefore you're creating more positive energy.

Combining the Elements

Enhance the chi in both the Relationship sector and the Helpful People sector at the same time. Because a different element represents each sector, using two elements together can amplify your chances for creating very strong relationships with those people in your work world.

For example, a lively plant in rich soil (Earth element) placed in a brass container (Metal element) enhances the chi in both the Helpful People and the Relationship sector. Doing so is otherwise known as a "two-fer." (If you thought that the brass container in this example should be round, which symbolizes Metal, or square, which symbolizes Earth, then you win a chi gold star! Both choices further enhance good chi.)

Picturing Your Work Place

Place a picture of your co-workers in the Relationship or Helpful People sector. Include photography of those people that you come in contact with most often and that shows them doing something pleasant, perhaps attending a company picnic.

If it occurred to you that putting the picture in a metal frame would enhance the chi, you're right! (You get another chi gold star.) If you realized that putting a picture of your boss in the Helpful People sector would improve your relationship with him or her, another gold star! (Just don't let your co-workers think you're brown-nosing the boss.) Use a photo that shows your boss and co-workers. Take a special photo if you have to.

Coloring Your Space

The color associated with the Helpful People sector is silver or gray shading toward black (but not black itself, which symbolizes the Career sector). The color associated with the Relationship sector is yellow for co-workers. (Use pink for romantic relationships, and unless you're carrying on with your co-workers, leave pink at home.) By adding silver and yellow to your workspace, you can enhance your relationships with your fellow employees.

Raising Chi with Cures

You can increase the chi in the Relationship sector or the Helpful People sector by using the cures we describe throughout the book. Mirrors, wind chimes, and crystals are all powerful cures that can help improve your relationships with others. Chapter 2 has an abundance of chi information.

Creating Comfortable Positions

In negotiations, you want to choose the power position — the position where you're facing the door, your back is to the wall (supported), and you're facing a favorable direction. To further strengthen your empowerment allows the other party to take a less supported position — back to the door or a window, and in a smaller chair across the desk from you.

But this type of power positioning won't improve your relationships with your co-workers. Instead, choose positions that indicate cooperation. For example, sit with your co-workers at a round table. Don't force others to sit with their backs to the door, making them feel vulnerable. Create positions of equal strength.

Understanding the Animal in Us All

The Chinese zodiac contains 12 animals, each with different attributes. Some of the animals are compatible with one another and others are antagonistic to each other. (Others are more neutral — they can have reasonable and workable relationships with one another.) See Chapter 1 for a further explanation of the zodiac and to identify your celestial animal.

You can't do anything about the sign you or your co-workers were born under, but by understanding the influence that signs can have on people's personalities, you may at least have an explanation for that otherwise hard-to-understand animosity you and the guy in the cubicle next door have for one another.

Chapter 19

Ten Ways to Get Yourself into a Power Position

In This Chapter

▶ Understanding power positions

▶ Arranging your work area to enhance your power positions

I n Feng Shui, you can create favorable conditions for yourself and your goals by taking advantage of power positions — that is, choosing to place yourself physically in such a way that you communicate power on a subtle, energetic level.

By creating personal power through Feng Shui, you can encourage others to see things your way, and persuade them to support you and your career goals. Personal power should not be misused to harm other people, but instead used to enrich yourself without hurting others and to gather support from those around you.

When you have the opportunity, using Feng Shui to design your workspace makes sense so that you create as much personal power as possible. Create power by trying the following tips in this chapter, all of which work for any situation in which you must choose a sitting position. (They also work when you're standing.)

So whether you're in a business meeting away from home or in the third-floor conference room, keep these principles in mind and you can create more personal power. This chapter gives you the tools to have the upper hand in bargaining and negotiating and conveys the subtle message that you're a confident person.

Facing It: Your Best Direction, That Is

If possible, place your desk so that you face your most auspicious direction (see Chapter 1 to determine what this is). This creates much more personal power than if you don't face your most favorable direction. Remember, while you have only one "most favorable" direction, you do have several directions that are favorable for you, so if you can't face the most favorable, try the second-most-favorable direction.

Seeing the Door

Having your desk face your most auspicious direction can help create personal power. But it's more important to have your desk face the door (or workspace entrance) than to have it face your most auspicious direction. If you have to choose between the two, choose to have your desk face the door. If for some reason you can't position your desk facing the door, place a mirror above your workspace so that you can see the door while you're seated.

Pointing Your Desk In the Right Direction

Although your desk should face the door or workspace entrance, it shouldn't be placed directly in front of the door or in a direct path from the door. The best position is for your desk to be as far from the door as possible without leaving the room, and placed to one side or the other of the path from the entrance. This allows you to see who is entering your space and gives you time to prepare to engage with them, instead of having them suddenly in your face.

Having Your Back Against a Wall Is Good

Sit with your back to a wall to give added energetic support to your position. Windows and doors can make you feel or appear vulnerable, and since you're not facing them, any potential threat comes from behind, where you can't see it. This can make you feel weaker on an energetic level. See Chapter 8 for more information about desk positioning.

Sitting in the Big Kids' Chair

Chief Executive Officers think that bigger is better: bigger cars, bigger corporate jets, bigger expense accounts. . . So it's no wonder they choose to sit in those big executive chairs. Size can make you appear more powerful. One way to create such size in your office is to sit in a slightly larger chair or in a more elevated position than others in the room. You can choose a desk chair that's larger than the guest chairs in your workspace. When you have to select a chair in another environment, choose the big one with arms rather than the dinky folding chair along the wall.

Your Office from 10,000 Feet

Ensure that you can see as much of the room/workspace as possible from your seated position. This makes you feel in control and therefore more powerful. In other words, no surprises will be creeping up on you!

Going to the Head of the Class

When choosing a position at a conference table or in a classroom setting, go to the head of the table or the room. When you're finding a place around a rectangular conference table, choose either end (if these places haven't already been assigned to someone else). The guy in Figure 19-1 did and see how powerful *he* looks! The head of the table is a symbolically powerful position; by selecting it, you're choosing power. The power position is farthest from the door, where you're able to see the door, but can't look directly out the door. When taking a seat in a classroom, the chairs in the front row are symbolically for good strong students. Even if you don't qualify, sit in one of those chairs anyway: You might surprise yourself at how quickly you become a good strong student.

Figure 19-1: This guy is seated in the power position.

First in Line, First in Mind

If you're presenting a speech or meeting someone important and you're only one of many people, try to be either first or last in line. Others will remember the first person they saw, and they will remember the last person they saw, but they may not remember everyone in between. Be bold and go to the head of the line; or be courteous, and allow everyone else to go before you, but don't be average and find yourself in the unmemorable middle position.

Slipping into Some Strength

You can create personal power by creating a career wardrobe that projects an image of yourself that you'd like others to perceive. Essentially, no hard and fast rules exist on how to create Feng Shui balance in what you wear, so do it your own way. Find clothing that makes you feel confident and powerful. Develop a wardrobe of clothing that helps you create personal power. See Chapter 15 for more information about developing a powerful wardrobe.

Stating Your Intentions

The most important way to create personal power is to state your intentions. What do you hope to gain by creating this power? More success in your career? A better balance between work and family life? A big fat raise? Remind yourself of your intentions each time you put yourself in a power position. Then, even if you can't grab that seat at the head of the table, you can project the feeling that you ARE at the head of the table.

Appendix

Your Workspace Sketch Pad

● ●

*T*o make your life easier, we've included a sample workspace
sketch and some blank workspace for you to fill in with
sketches of your workspace, your Mom's workspace, a doodle, or
whatever! Check out Figure AA01 for an example and then go crazy
on the following pages. If your workspace isn't a perfect square like
those pictured here, you're welcome to alter as needed.

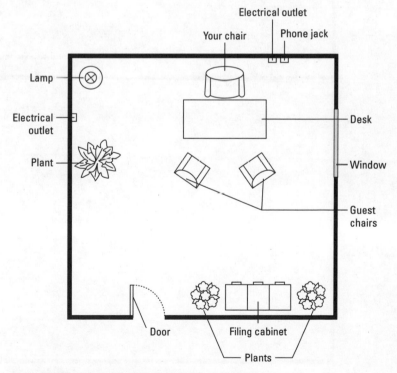

Figure AA01: A sample workspace for you to look at.

Sketch Your Workspace

Sketch Your Workspace

Sketch Your Workspace

Sketch Your Workspace

Sketch Your Workspace

Index

Notes

Notes

Notes

Notes

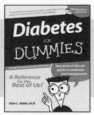

FOR DUMMIES®

Plain-English solutions for everyday challenges

COMPUTER BASICS

0-7645-0838-5

0-7645-1663-9

0-7645-1548-9

BUSINESS SOFTWARE

0-7645-0822-9

0-7645-0839-3

0-7645-0819-9

Get smart! Visit www.dummies.com

- **Find listings of even more *For Dummies* titles**
- **Browse online articles**
- **Sign up for Dummies eTips™**
- **Check out *For Dummies* fitness videos and other products**
- **Order from our online bookstore**

Available wherever books are sold. Go to www.dummies.com or call 1-877-762-2974 to order direct.

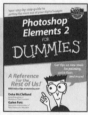

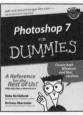

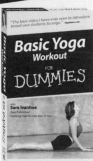

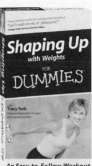
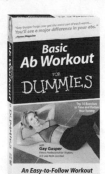

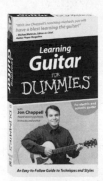